Study Guide
Volume 1

Western Civilization

SEVENTH EDITION

Jackson J. Spielvogel
The Pennsylvania State University

Prepared by

James T. Baker
Western Kentucky University

THOMSON

WADSWORTH

Australia • Brazil • Canada • Mexico • Singapore • Spain • United Kingdom • United States

ISBN-13: 978-0-495-56655-7
ISBN-10: 0-495-56655-1

Thomson Higher Education
25 Thomson Place
Boston, MA 02210
USA

For more information about our products, contact us at:
Thomson Learning Academic Resource Center
1-800-423-0563

For permission to use material from this text or product, submit a request online at
http://www.thomsonrights.com.
Any additional questions about permissions can be submitted by email to **thomsonrights@thomson.com.**

CONTENTS

PREFACE

This study guide is a companion volume to the text *Western Civilization* by Jackson J. Spielvogel. For each chapter it provides you with an outline, summary of contents, list of learning objectives, and glossary of important terms. Then it offers seven types of exercises that will enable you to examine your understanding of the materials in each chapter.

1. Words to Match with their Definitions---10 per chapter, a way to test your understanding of other significant terms
2. Multiple Choice Questions---20 per chapter, a way to test your factual and conceptual comprehension of the chapter's contents
3. Sentences to Complete---10 per chapter, with spaces provided for you to finish an interpretive statement with specific words and phrases
4. Chronological Arrangement---7 per chapter, an exercise in which you place event in chronological order and give their dates to test your understanding of time lines
5. Questions for Critical Thought---8 per chapter, questions that enable you to recall and explain important concepts in preparation for essay examinations
6. Analysis of Primary Source Documents---questions that ask you to interpret the meaning and significance of each primary document in the chapter
7. Map Exercises---which test your knowledge of geographical regions and specific places important to the historical period under review

You may check your completed maps with the appropriate ones in the text. Answers to exercises 1, 2, 3, and 4 are found at the end of the guide.

You will probably be asked on your examinations to write essays. Essays not only test your knowledge of the facts but your ability to interpret and apply them. The exercises in this volume called Questions for Critical Thought and Analysis of Primary Source Documents will be of help to you to prepare for essay questions. In addition, let me offer you several suggestions on how to write essays successfully.

1. Read the entire question, to be sure that you understand exactly what you are being asked to do and that you are aware of its various parts. Address yourself only to the question that is asked, but address every subdivision of it.

2. Make an outline before you begin to write the essay. Jot down in as few words as possible the major points you want to make and the most important persons, places, and ideas you want to include. Then glance back at your outline as you write so that you will not stay too long on any one point or omit any important points.

3. Make one major point in your essay, with all of the others subordinate to it. This is your thesis. State it at the beginning, refer back to it at various appropriate times, and restate it briefly at the end. This will keep you focused on a unifying theme.

4. Write for an imaginary reader who is intelligent but does not necessarily know the information you are relating. This way you will not fail to provide all information necessary to explain yourself, but you will also not insult your reader.

5. Spell correctly and use good grammar. A history course is not an English course, and graders may or may not "count off" for poor spelling and grammar; but all graders are impressed either positively or negatively by the quality of your writing. While you may not see a specific comment about your spelling and grammar on your essay when it is returned, you may be sure that they have affected your final grade.

6. Adopt a positive attitude toward writing your essay. It can and should help you understand better the facts you have learned and make them a permanent part of your historical knowledge. If done correctly, an essay can be a pleasant and valuable learning experience.

I hope that this study guide adds to your enjoyment of the study of Western Civilization, increases your understanding of the ages you study, and helps you achieve high marks.

James T. Baker

CHAPTER 1
THE ANCIENT NEAR EAST:
THE FIRST CIVILIZATIONS

Chapter Outline

I. First Humans
    A. Hunter-Gatherers of the Old Stone Age
        1. Nomads
        2. Caves
        3. Tools and Fire
    B. Neolithic Revolution (c.10,000-4,000 B.C.)
        1. Agricultural Revolution
        2. Farming Villages
        3. Homes and Families
        4. Technological Advances

II. Emergence of Civilization
    A. Urban Life
    B. Religious Structures
    C. Political and Military Structures
    D. Socio-economic Structures
    E. Writing
    F. Artistic and Intellectual Activities
    G. Civilizations in Mesopotamia, India, China, and South America

III. Civilization in Mesopotamia
    A. City-States of Ancient Mesopotamia
        1. Sumerians
        2. Kingship and Religion
        3. Economy and Society
    B. Mesopotamian Empires
        1. Sumer
        2. Akkadian Empire and Sargon
        3. Babylon and Hammurabi
    C. Hammurabi's Code
        1. "An Eye for an Eye"
        2. Responsibilities of Public Officials
        3. Consumer Protection
        4. Commerce
        5. Women
        6. Sex and the Family

D. Mesopotamian Culture
    1. Religion
        a. *Enuma elish* and Marduk
        b. Ziggurats
        c. The Power of Nature
        d. Polytheism
        e. Divination
    2. Writing
        a. Cuneiform
        b. Record-keeping
    3. Literature: *Epic of Gilgamesh*
    4. Mathematics and Astronomy

IV. Egyptian Civilization: "The Gift of the Nile"
    A. The Nile River
    B. Natural Barriers
    C. Old and Middle Kingdoms
        1. Old Kingdom
            a. Kingship and the Two Crowns
            b. *Ma'at* (Right Order and Harmony)
            c. Nomes (Provinces)
        2. Middle Kingdom
            a. Order out of Chaos
            b. Pharaoh as Shepherd
            c. Expansion
    D. Society and Economy
        1. Nobles and Priests
        2. Merchants and Artisans
        3. Farmers
    E. Egyptian Culture
        1. Spiritual Life
            a. Atum-Re
            b. Osiris and Isis
            c. *Book of the Dead*
        2. Pyramids
            a. Preservation of the Pharaohs
            b. Great Pyramid at Giza
        3. Art and Writing
            a. Formulaic Painting
            b. Hieroglyphics
    F. Disorder and a New Order
        1. Hyksos
        2. New Kingdom: Egyptian Empire
            a. Ahmose I
            b. Tuthmosis III
            c. Amenhotep III
            d. Amenhotep IV and Aten
            e. Rameses II

G. Daily Life in Ancient Egypt
    1. Home and Family
    2. Women: Hatshepsut
    3. Material Abundance
    4. Entertainment

V. On the Fringes of Civilization
    A. Megaliths (Stonehenge)
    B. Indo-Europeans (The Hittites)

Chapter Summary

The people of the Western world share a common cultural heritage with people the world over. They certainly share the prehistoric periods of human development, when men and women learned to use stone tools, domesticate plants and animals, and live together in settled communities. Out of these experiences common to all *homo sapiens sapiens*, Western man emerged as civilized man, with all the characteristics common to civilizations: writing, religion, art, and law.

Western civilization, with its various cultural forms, was born in the Near East; and there it traces its origins to two distinct roots. One of these was what the later Greeks called the "land between the rivers," Mesopotamia, which lies within the "fertile crescent" that runs from what is today Israel on the Mediterranean Sea to Kuwait on the Persian Gulf, with its center in what is today Iraq. The civilization of Mesopotamia developed a complete code of law under King Hammurabi, a literature written in cuneiform with stories of creation and a great flood, and virtually indestructible buildings where they worshipped a multitude of gods.

The other root was Egypt. A land born of and dominated by the Nile River, Egypt developed a civilization based upon royal power and centralized government as well as deep spiritual sensitivities. Its sacred script, hieroglyphics, captured and transmitted a complex and colorful body of literature and philosophy. Its gigantic architecture and art, particularly that which served to glorify and amplify the lives and deaths of pharaohs, continue to impress visitors thousands of years after their completion. By its influence over Greek, Roman, and Arab imitators and transmitters, Egyptian civilization also helped to mold Western civilization.

To discover and study these roots is to expand both the age and horizons of Western civilization. It enables us who are inheritors to see that while our culture is neither original nor unique, we have given our own particular interpretation and flavor to a civilization common to all humanity.

Learning Objectives

1. Be able to describe the nature and historical significance of the agricultural revolution in the Neolithic period.

2. Be able to detail what the city-states of Mesopotamia contributed to the development of Western civilization.

3. Be able to describe the most important characteristics of Mesopotamian culture. Explain how these characteristics developed and how they influenced later historical eras.

4. Be able to demonstrate the importance of the Nile River to the historical, social, and historical development of ancient Egypt.

5. Be able to discuss the major characteristics of the religion of ancient Egypt. Be able to explain how Egypt's religious practices developed and how they reflected Egyptian culture as a whole.

Glossary of Names and Terms

1. *Homo sapiens*: the species of humankind that rose in Africa over 150,000 years ago; spread to every part of the globe; and by 10,000 B.C. was the only species of humans left on earth.

2. Mesopotamia: literally "the land between the rivers" (the Tigris and Euphrates), the place where Western civilization was born, located in what is today Iraq.

3. Hammurabi: Amorite king (1792-1750 B.C.) who reunited Mesopotamia; founded a famous capital at Babylon; and codified the various and sundry laws of the region.

4. Gilgamesh: a Mesopotamian king famous as the hero of a great epic tale in which he battles a great beast named Enkidu, makes peace with him, and goes with him in search of immortality.

5. *Ma'at*: The Egyptian philosophical principle of truth and justice, which the pharaohs were expected to apply to their attempts to create an orderly and harmonious society.

6. Osiris: a leader who brought civilization to Egypt; was killed by his jealous brother Seth; and was resurrected by his wife Isis.

7. Hieroglyphics: the "sacred writing" of the Egyptian priests, composed of stylized pictures, preserved on stone monuments, wood panels, and papyrus rolls.

8. Amenhotep IV: Egyptian pharaoh who introduced a new religion, the worship of one god, Aten, and moved the capital in order to escape the power of other religions.

9. Hatshepsut: female pharaoh who proved an aggressive leader in warfare and economic enterprises, always shown in statues dressed in men's clothing and wearing a beard.

10. Stonehenge: the most famous example of a prehistoric megalith, located in southeastern England, and demonstrating a sophisticated understanding of astronomy and social organization.

Match these Words with their Definitions

1. Australopithecines

2. Paleolithic

3. Enlil

4. Polytheism

5. Enkidu

6. Re

7. Osiris

8. Giza

9. Hyksos

10. Thutmosis III

A. Belief in and worship of multiple gods

B. Site of Egypt's Great Pyramid

C. Symbol of resurrection

D. Sumerian god of the wind and the proper use of force

E. Desert people who introduced the war chariot to Egypt

F. Earliest period of man's development

G. Pharaoh under whose rule Egypt conquered Palestine

H. Egyptian god of the sun who had the head of a falcon

I. First hominids to use stone tools

J. "Hairy beast" of Mesopotamian mythology, Gilgamesh's fast friend

Choose the Correct Answer

1. All of the following are believed to be achievements of the Paleolithic Age *except*

    a. The utilization of tools
    b. Development of abstract thought
    c. Development of art
    d. The regular production of food through agriculture
    e. A rough equality between men and women

2. Neolithic social patterns that proved to be enduring were
    a. A division of labor based on gender
    b. Establishment of fixed dwellings
    c. The domestication of animals
    d. Crafts using metal
    e. All of the above

3. Which of the following is *not* considered a characteristic of civilization, especially as the term applies to ancient Mesopotamia and Egypt?

    a. Organized political structures and government bureaucracies
    b. A social structure based on democratic principles
    c. Development of writing and written records
    d. Religious structures in which priests were vital to the community's success
    e. Urban centers

4. The forces of nature in ancient Mesopotamia made the people feel

    a. Optimistic about the future
    b. Doomed and without hope
    c. Dependent upon the gods for survival
    d. Sunny and carefree
    e. Science could solve all human problems

5. Which of the following is *not* true of Mesopotamian society?

    a. Commerce and industry were important, second only to agriculture
    b. Small villages, without defensive walls, were the basic units of civilization
    c. Slaves were on the whole well treated
    d. The economy was divided into both public and private sectors
    e. The most prominent structures were temples

6. The Code of Hammurabi sought to achieve all of the following *except*

    a. Equality of the sexes
    b. Financial liability
    c. Military stability
    d. Commercial integrity
    e. Stable sexual relationships

7. The Code of Hammurabi

    a. Abolished the old class system
    b. Established order through a well-understood set of laws
    c. Had little to do with criminal law
    d. Inspired fear in the general populace
    e. Gave women equal status with men

8. Hammurabi's code contained specific regulations on

    a. Marriage
    b. Adultery
    c. Incest
    d. Divorce
    e. All of the above

9. The Ziggurats of Mesopotamia were used for

    a. Games and other urban recreation
    b. Sacrifices to the king
    c. Worship of the city's god
    d. Military training
    e. Vocational training

10. The *Epic of Gilgamesh* teaches that

    a. The gods are benevolent and care greatly for people
    b. A wish that is fulfilled is not always a good thing
    c. Everlasting life is reserved only for the gods
    d. A periodic flood is necessary to keep the world pure
    e. People of different classes cannot make lasting friendships

11. The "prophet" Neferti described Egypt at the collapse of the Old Kingdom as a society

    a.   Obsessed with monotheistic religious fervor
    b.   Facing a severe shortage of water
    c.   Weakened by a strain of idiocy in the royal family
    d.   Wrecked by the invasion of desert barbarians
    e.   Weakened to the point of exhaustion by civil wars

12. The Egyptian god Osiris eventually came to be identified as

    a.   Father-King of the sky
    b.   Judge of the dead
    c.   The incarnation of pharaoh
    d.   The Hebrew messiah
    e.   A false deity introduced to confuse the people

13. The Second Intermediate period of Egyptian history was marked by

    a.   The rise of rival local dynasties
    b.   The adoption of a new language due to long domination by the Hyksos
    c.   New methods in agriculture introduced by the Hyksos
    d.   An increase in the number of foreign wars
    e.   A decline in religious devotion

14. The Hyksos, a tribe of foreigners who ruled Egypt, came originally from the

    a.   Arabian desert
    b.   Hellenic islands
    c.   Eastern shores of the Persian Gulf
    d.   Mountains of Central Africa
    e.   Coasts of the Dead Sea

15. Which of the following is *not* true of Egyptian art?

    a.   It permitted great individual artists to distinguish themselves
    b.   It was primarily functional
    c.   It was highly stylized
    d.   It followed strict formulas
    e.   It accurately represented each part of the human form

16. Which of the following is true of Egyptian art or literature?

    a.   The system of hieroglyphics was the precursor of the Western alphabet
    b.   Wall paintings in pharaohs' tombs had specific functional purposes
    c.   Art seldom showed distinctive features of subjects
    d.   Literature centered around fantastic tales of fictional characters
    e.   Literature seldom had religious themes

17. Which of the following is *not* true of women in Egypt?

    a. They could hold inherited property, even in marriage
    b. Queens could have more than one husband
    c. They could be pharaohs
    d. Upper class women could be priests
    e. They could operate businesses

18. An Egyptian boy, when writing to his sweetheart, would typically address her as

    a. Beloved one
    b. Sister
    c. Treasured virgin
    d. Maiden
    e. Promised one

19. Stonehenge demonstrates remarkable early human knowledge and skill in

    a. Astronomy
    b. Transport of heavy materials
    c. Engineering
    d. Coordination of labor
    e. All of the above

20. The term "Indo-European" when describing a people refers to

    a. A grouping of languages
    b. Artistic styles of a primitive form
    c. Types of megaliths
    d. Religious principles and practices
    e. Skull size and shape

Complete the Following Sentences

1. Çatal Hüyük, an ancient city located in what is today _____, shows that by 6000 B.C. man could produce food _____ and had time to make _____ and _____.

2. Because its rivers were unpredictable, farming in Mesopotamia was possible only by _____ and digging _____ _____.

3. Mesopotamian city-states may first have been ruled by _____ before later ruled by _____.

4. Punishment under Hammurabi's Code was often _____ and varied according to the _____ _____ of the victim.

5. The regular floods of the Nile gave Egyptian society a sense of _____ and led to a _____ rather than a linear view of history.

6. Ancient Egypt's Old Kingdom had _____ dynasties, the Middle Kingdom had _____, and the New Kingdom had _____.

7. During the Old Kingdom, Egypt was divided into administrative districts which later Greek historians called _____, administered by _____, who were required to obey the _____ and his _____.

8. Egypt's judge of the dead was the god _____, killed by his evil brother _____ and restored to life by the actions of his sister _____.

9. The largest pyramids were built during Egypt's _____ kingdom. The Great Pyramid of Khufu was built at _____ around _____ B.C.

10. Since Pharaohs were mostly men, the female Pharaoh Hatshepsut was addressed as ___ _____ and was portrayed in statuary wearing men's clothing and a _____.

Place the Following in Chronological Order and Give Approximate Dates

1. Building of Tell-el-Amarna   1.

2. Reign of Tuhtmosis III   2.

3. Civilized life at Çatal Hüyük   3.

4. Code of Hammurabi   4.

5. Building of the Great Pyramid of Giza   5.

6. Hyksos Invasion of Egypt   6.

7. Construction of Stonehenge   7.

Questions for Critical Thought

1. What are the main characteristics of a civilization? What are the alternatives to civilization? Why do humans prefer civilization to the alternatives?

2. Discuss the civilization that arose in Mesopotamia: its economic, social, and political systems. Why did this civilization develop when and where it did; and what did it leave the world when it came to an end?

3. What part did religion play in Mesopotamian culture? Why was religion so important to the people there, what forms did it take, and what did Mesopotamian religion pass on to succeeding civilizations?

4. Describe the Code of Hammurabi. What problems did it address, and what penalties did it impose on those who broke the laws? In what ways do you as a modern person find this code to be just and/or unjust?

5. Discuss the achievements of Mesopotamian literature. What were its concerns, its subjects, and the forms it adopted? What patterns did it set for writers in later cultures?

6. List the major features of the Egyptian political system, religious establishment, and social structure. How did the three work together to create a harmonious civilization? How has Egyptian civilization contributed to subsequent civilizations?

7. How were the two major religious traditions of Egypt molded by the geography of the land? Why did one form of religion find favor among the royal family, while quite another was popular with the masses?

8. Describe daily life in Egypt: working, family life, worship, entertainment, the hunt. What were the strengths and weaknesses of this society?

Analysis of Primary Source Documents

1. What do the twelve laws from the Code of Hammurabi tell you about the nature and concerns of this king and his people? Why do historians use the phrase "an eye for an eye, a tooth for a tooth" to describe his code?

2. What does the Mesopotamian creation myth tell you about that culture's assumptions about the nature of the gods and man?

3. Describe the typical day of a Sumerian school boy. What did he learn, both formally and informally? What sort of an adult was he likely to become?

4. Compare the flood story of the *Gilgamesh Epic* to the more familiar Biblical account. How does the Biblical account follow and how does it deviate from the older story?

5. Use the "Hymn to the Nile" to illustrate the importance of that river to Egypt. In what sense did the Egyptians consider it divine? Speculate on how the "Hymn to Pharaoh" might have been performed. Where, by whom, and in what dramatic form was it likely sung and acted?

6. What qualities did Akhenaten attribute to his new god? How might Egypt's culture have been changed had Akhenaten's religious revolution succeeded? What connection do you think might exist between the *Hymn to Aten* and *Psalm 104*?

7. What assumptions and values underlie Any's advice on how to treat a woman? Were Egyptian women valued only for their child-bearing? Were they equal to men?

8. Using the advice the vizier gave his son, describe the way an Egyptian official was expected to behave. How do you suppose this young man took such advice? Did Egyptian society make sons submissive, or could this one have been inwardly rebellious?

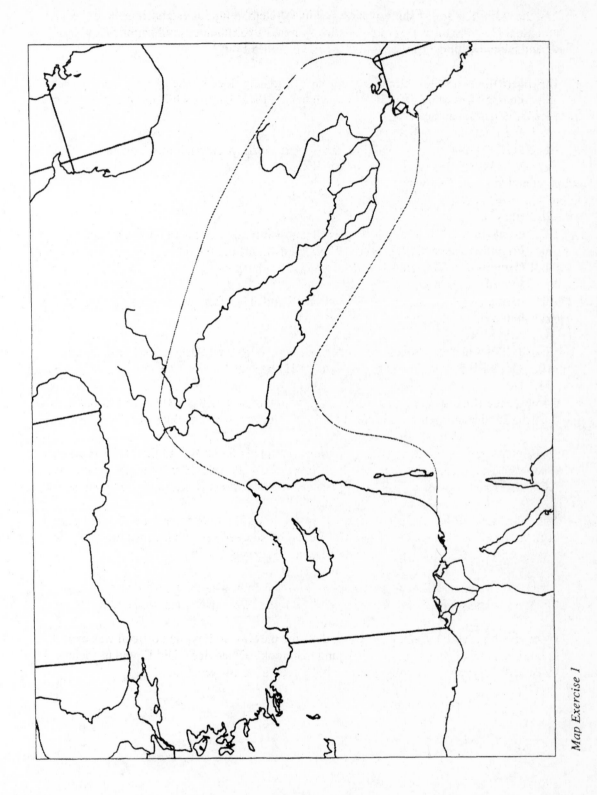

Chapter 1

Map Exercise 1: The Ancient Near East

Shade and label the following

    1. Egypt
    2. Fertile Crescent
    3. Mediterranean Sea
    4. Mesopotamia
    5. Persian Gulf

Pinpoint and label the following

    1. Babylon
    2. Çatal Hüyük
    3. Euphrates River
    4. Giza
    5. Jerusalem
    6. Memphis
    7. Nineveh
    8. Nile River
    9. Tell-el-Amarna
    10. Tigris River
    11. Ur

CHAPTER 2
THE ANCIENT NEAR EAST:
PEOPLES AND EMPIRES

Chapter Outline

I.   The Hebrews: "Children of Israel"
  A.   United Kingdom
    1.   Saul, the First King
    2.   David and Jerusalem
    3.   Solomon and the Temple
  B.   Divided Kingdom: Captivity and Return
  C.   Spiritual Dimensions of Israel
    1.   Yahweh: Ruler of the World
    2.   Covenant, Law, and Prophets
  D.   Social Structure of the Hebrews
    1.   Men of Rank and Influence
    2.   Marriage and the Family
    3.   Men and Women

II.   The Neighbors of the Israelites
  A.   Explorers to the West
  B.   Alphabet

III.   The Assyrian Empire
  A.   Tiglath-Pileser
  B.   Ashurbanipal
  C.   Organization of the Empire
  D.   Military Machine
  E.   Society and Culture
    1.   Free and Non-free
    2.   Agriculture and Trade
    3.   Relief Sculpture

IV.   The Neo-Babylonian Empire
  A.   Nebuchadnezzar II
  B.   Grand City of Babylon

V.   The Persian Empire
  A.   Medes
  B.   Cyrus the Great
    1.   Control of Media
    2.   Conquest of Lydia
    3.   Victory over Babylon
    4.   Freedom for the Hebrews

      C.   Expanding the Empire
          1. Cambyses
          2. Darius
          3. Confrontation with the Greeks
      D.   Governing the Empire
          1. Satrapies
          2. Communication and Transportation
      E.   Darius: The Great King
      E.   Persian Religion
          1. Zoroaster and Zoroasterism
          2. Dualism: Ahuramazda and Ahriman
          3. Mithra and Mithraism

Chapter Summary

Christianity---eventually the dominant religious faith of the West---was in large part a child of the Hebrew religion. It is therefore necessary to study the Hebrews in order to understand Western civilization. Their Bible, which Christians call the Old Testament, contains both the history and the religious thought of the Hebrews.

The Old Testament explains how the Hebrew god, Yahweh, made a covenant with the sons of Abraham and gave his "chosen people" a set of laws by which to live. The story of the chosen people, who came eventually to be called Jews, moves from their origin in Mesopotamia to slavery in Egypt to nationhood in Palestine to a second exile in Mesopotamia and back home again. Their founders gave them the law; their prophets taught them how to apply it to society; their psalmists composed hymns to celebrate it; and their theologians taught them various ways to interpret it. For Christians the most significant Jewish figure was Jesus of Nazareth.

The Hebrews did not, however, live in isolation. They first came to their promised land, Palestine, from ancient Mesopotamia. They returned to Palestine once from Egyptian slavery and again from exile in Babylon. They borrowed culturally both from Egyptian society to the south and from Mesopotamian culture to the east. They were particularly influenced, both positively and negatively, by what they considered their mother country and the succession of empires that ruled it: Assyria with its great collection of literature and history; Babylon with its hanging gardens, broad avenues, and militant gods; and perhaps most of all by Persia with its father-king Cyrus, its concept of world government, and its Zoroastrian religion, which featured a battle between the forces of good and evil.

Much of what we learn about the ancient Near East sounds familiar to Westerners because Western civilization itself borrowed so heavily from the peoples of that time and place we mistakenly think of as so far away.

Learning Objectives

1.   Be able to show how the Hebrews created their "united kingdom" and why it later became the "divided kingdom."

2.   Be able to outline the major religious ideas that made the Hebrews a specific people and the ritual practices they created to celebrate those ideas.

3.   Be able to account for the great military conquests of the Assyrian Empire.

4. Be able to explain the organization and leadership that made the Persian Empire so successful for such a long period of time.

5. Be able to list the main tenets of Zoroastrianism and how they influenced other religions, including Judaism and Christianity.

Glossary of Names and Terms

1. Exodus: the "departure" of the "children of Israel" from bondage in Egypt, a movement led by the heroic figure Moses in the first half of the thirteenth century B.C.

2. David: the second king of the Hebrew nation, the leader who created a central administration, brought much of Palestine under Hebrew control, and made Jerusalem its capital.

3. Solomon: the son of David, who as king of the United Hebrew Kingdom brought the nation to the heights of its economic power and built the first temple in Jerusalem.

4. Yahweh: the name of the Hebrews' protector, the God who gave them their law, the Being they came to believe was the only true God and ruler of the world.

5. Covenant: the agreement the Hebrews believed they had made with Yahweh, making them his "chosen people," which required them to follow Yahweh's law and gave them a special place in history.

6. Prophets: Hebrew "holy men" who called on the nation to follow the divine law, warned them of dire consequences if they did not, and helped make Judaism a universal religion.

7. Cyrus: the Persian king who brought most of the near east under one government, a man whose mercy to conquered peoples earned him widespread respect and earned him the title "Cyrus the Great."

8. Satrapies: administrative divisions of the Persian Empire, organized to solve local problems but subservient to the central government, inspected by visitors called "the king's eyes."

9. Zoroaster: semi-legendary founder of Persia's most influential religion, which emphasized an ongoing struggle between good and bad divinities.

10. Ahuramazda: the true or good god of Zoroastrianism, opponent of the evil god Ahriman, the eventual victor in the battle for supremacy, final judge of men.

Chapter 2

Match these Words with their Definitions

1. Moses

2. David

3. Babylon

4. Amos

5. *Proverbs*
6. Phoenicians

7. Nineveh

8. Cambyses

9. Persepolis

10. Zoroaster

A. Contains a description of the ideal Hebrew wife

B. Persian conqueror of Egypt

C. Its fall brought the Assyrian Empire to an end

D. Semi-legendary Persian religious teacher

E. Creators of the alphabet that was eventually adopted by the western world

F. Darius' new capital that replaced Susa

G. Site of the second Hebrew captivity

H. Made Jerusalem the Hebrew capital

I. Prophesied the fall of Israel

J. Leader of the Hebrew exodus from Egyptian slavery

Choose the Correct Answer

1. The early books of the Bible describe

    a. The creation of man and woman
    b. The covenant with Abraham
    c. The exodus from Egypt
    d. The giving of the Mosaic Law
    e. All of the above

2. The chronological chain of Hebrew leadership was

    a. Moses, Saul, David, Solomon, Ahab
    b. Moses, David, Solomon, Saul, Ahab
    c. Saul, David, Solomon, Ahab, Nebuchadnezzar
    d. Moses, Solomon, Ahab, Nebuchadnezzar, Saul
    e. David, Solomon, Saul, Ashurbanipal

3. The Hebrew concept of Yahweh as God led to all but which of the following:

    a. The establishment of the Torah
    b. Polytheistic Rituals
    c. A Covenant between God and people
    d. The rise of prophets
    e. A feeling of being a "chosen" people

4. All of the following are true concerning the fully developed Hebrew concept of God *except*

    a. He was the creator of but not an inherent part of nature
    b. All peoples of the world were subject to him
    c. He was a compassionate and loving father, though he would punish those who disobeyed him
    d. His stern nature left no room for personal contact with him
    e. He considered the Hebrews his "chosen" people

5. The prophets played a crucial role in Hebrew society by

    a. Dominating political as well as spiritual thought
    b. Preaching only optimistic messages
    c. Calling attention to social injustices
    d. Leading Hebrew armies into battle
    e. Drawing up explicit blueprints for the Temple

6. The prophets preached all of the following *except* that Yahweh

    a. Was the God only of the Hebrews
    b. Was the universal divinity
    c. Hated Hebrew class distinctions
    d. Would use foreign nations to punish his people
    e. Watched over his people even in exile

7. The dominant theme of the Hebrew Bible is

   a. Sacrificial offerings
   b. Loyalty to the Nation of Israel
   c. The mystery of an unknowable God
   d. Obedience to God seen in historical events
   e. Jewish racial superiority

8. The last profession to develop in Hebrew society was that of

   a. Soldier
   b. Merchant
   c. Priest
   d. Scholar
   e. Shepherd

9. *Proverbs'* description of an ideal wife mentions all the following *except* her

   a. Business acumen
   b. Tireless physical labor
   c. Compassion for the poor
   d. Devotion to daily prayers
   e. Husband's respect

10. Hebrew education was designed primarily to

    a. Provide moral instruction and train boys for a trade
    b. Prepare men for war and women for housework
    c. Train young men for the office of rabbi
    d. Make the Hebrew nation fully literate
    e. Assure that there would be poets and architects

11. While the Phoenicians traded widely, the only colony where they sent families to settle was

    a. Bristol in southeastern Britain
    b. Carthage in North Africa
    c. Titlos on the Persian Gulf
    d. Sardinia in Italy
    e. Messina in southern Gaul

12. The Assyrian military machine was successful for all *but* which of these reasons

    a. Enormous numbers of soldiers
    b. Use of iron weapons
    c. Terror tactics
    d. Use of elephants in attacks
    e. Tight organization and discipline

13. The Assyrian capital Nineveh was known throughout the ancient world for its

    a. Mural paintings that depicted historical events
    b. Concert hall that seated 10,000 people
    c. Enormous library with literary works of all kinds
    d. Hanging gardens, called one of the Seven Wonders of the World
    e. Zoo with animals from every known part of the world

14. Assyrian art was best known for its

    a. Wall murals
    b. Free-standing sculpture
    c. Relief sculptures
    d. Gold leaf covered furniture
    e. Hand-painted artificial eggs

15. Which of the following statements is *not* true of the Neo-Babylonian Empire?

    a. Its founder was Nabopolassar
    b. It was the longest lasting of the ancient Near Eastern empires
    c. Its capital city Babylon had hanging gardens
    d. King Nabonidus emphasized the worship of Zoroaster rather than Marduk
    e. The residents of Babylon welcomed its fall to Persia

16. The Jews, who were in Babylonian exile when the Persian ruler Cyrus became their new master, regarded him as a

    a. Brutal dictator and pretender to the throne
    b. Cold-blooded butcher and terrorist
    c. Man anointed by their God
    d. Holy man who would reform religion
    e. Weak man who would not survive the civil wars that engulfed him

17. The Persian system of satrapies under Darius allowed for

    a. Subject peoples to play a dominant role in civil administration
    b. A sensible system of calculating how much tribute a region owed
    c. Offices with royal trappings to be filled by election rather than by birth
    d. Widespread corruption by the satraps, who could act without the emperor's knowledge
    e. The propagation of the Hebrew religion throughout the empire

18. One fatal weakness of later Persian kings, which eventually led to the decline of their empire, was their

    a. Congenital effeminacy
    b. Lust for wealth
    c. Harsh punishment of rebels
    d. Love of lavish banquets
    e. Tendency to change religions

19. The success of the Persian military machine was due in large part to its

    a. International character
    b. Constant replacement of fallen soldiers
    c. Effective use of cavalry behind enemy lines
    d. Use of ships taken from subjected countries
    e. All of the above

20. Which of the following statements about Zoroastrianism is *false*?

    a. It was dualistic
    b. It had great influence in the Persian Empire
    c. It had no doctrine of a final judgment
    d. Its supreme deity was Ahuramazda
    e. Its evil divinity was Ahriman

Complete the Following Sentences

1. Solomon's most famous contribution to Hebrew religion was construction of the _____ in Jerusalem, where the _____ of the _____ was kept.

2. The Hebrews were twice held in bondage, first in _____, later in _____. They were freed from the latter by the Persian king _____.

3. The Hebrew's believed their deity, whose name was _____, had made a formal _____ with them, under which they were to obey his _____.

4. The greatest international sea traders of the ancient Near East were the _____, who gave the Western world its _____.

5. The strong unifying focus of the hybrid Assyrian Empire was the _____, whose power was considered _____.

6. The Assyrian army was effective because of its weapons made of _____, its use of _____ warfare in the mountains, and because of its ability to _____ its enemies.

7. The Persian Empire of Cyrus reached its height by its conquest in order of _____, _____, the _____ Greeks, and finally _____.

8. The only region to escape the ambitions of Cyrus the Great was _____, but it was conquered by his son _____, who made its capital _____.

9. Persia reached its geographical zenith under _____, who moved the capital from _____ to _____.

10. The greatest Persian religious leader, _____, taught in his book of hymns, the _____, that the supreme deity _____ was engaged in a universal struggle with the god of evil, _____.

Place the Following in Chronological Order and Give Dates

1. Fall of Jerusalem and beginning of the   1.
    Babylonian Captivity

2. Reign of King David   2.

3. Northern Kingdom of Israel destroyed   3.
    by the Assyrians

4. Birth of Zoroaster   4.

5. Building of Solomon's temple   5.

6. Reign of Cyrus the Great in Persia   6.

7. Exodus of the Hebrews from Egypt   7.

Questions for Critical Thought

1. Describe the role of the Covenant and the Mosaic Law in the development of Hebrew religion and culture.

2. Discuss the part prophecy played in Hebrew history and social development.

3. Explain how the Hebrew faith was unique and what characteristics it shared with other religions of the Near East.

4. The family was the central social institution of the Hebrew community. Describe it, and speculate on how at the age you now are you would have adapted to your place in it.

5. Discuss the Phoenician contributions to Western civilization. Is it a major root or merely a branch among other branches?

6. Describe the political, military, and social organization of the Assyrian Empire. What influences did it have on subsequent Middle Eastern empires?

7. Explain why or why not the Persian emperor Cyrus deserves to be called by historians "Cyrus the Great"?

8. Describe the Zoroastrian religion. How did it change over time and what caused it to spread from Persia to so many other areas? Do any of its principles survive in modern religions?

Chapter 2

Analysis of Primary Source Documents

1. Describe the covenant Moses proclaimed between Yahweh and Israel. What were responsibilities and implications for each side?

2. What did the Hebrew prophets say would happen if God's chosen people did not fulfill their obligations under the covenant? In what sense were the Hebrews God's "chosen" people?

3. Analyze the claims Assyrian kings made about battle victories. To what extent do you feel these official claims were exaggerated? What would be the purpose of such exaggeration?

4. Explain the "wisdom" of Cyrus and the "foolishness" of the Babylonians in the Persian siege of Babylon. What military point was the Greek historian Herodotus trying to make?

5. Pretend you are a modern reporter who has been permitted to return through time to cover a Persian king's banquet. Describe to your twenty-first century readers what you see.

Chapter 3
The Civilization of the Greeks

Chapter Outline

I.   Early Greece
     A.   Role of Geography: Mountains and Sea
     B.   Minoan Crete
          1.   King Minos
          2.   The Palace at Knossus
     C.   First Greek State: Mycenaeans
          1.   Kings
          2.   Commerce
          3.   "Legend" of the Trojan War

II. The Greeks in a Dark Age (c.1100-c.750 B.C.)
     A.   Declines in Population and Farming
     B.   Coming of the Dorians
     C.   Homer's Stories of Glory
          1.   *The Iliad* (Battle for Troy)
          2.   *The Odyssey* (Wanderings of Odysseus)
     D.   Homer's Enduring Importance

III. World of the Greek City-States (750-500 B.C.)
     A.   Polis
     B.   Colonization and Growth of Trade
          1.   Reasons for Expansion
          2.   Varieties of Greek Colonies
          3.   Diffusion of Greek Culture
     C.   Tyranny in the Greek Polis
          1.   Power by Force
          2.   Strengthening of Economies and Cultural Expression
     D.   Example of Sparta
          1.   A Military State
          2.   Lycurgus the Law-giver
          3.   Spartan State and Society
     E.   Example of Athens
          1.   Reforms of Solon
          2.   "Mild Tyranny" of Pisistratus
          3.   Reforms of Cleisthenes
     F.   Greek Culture in the Archaic Age
          1.   *Kouros* Figures
          2.   Lyric Poetry
               a.   Sappho
               b.   Hesiod
               c.   Theognis

IV. The High Point of Greek Civilization: Classical Greece (500-338 B.C.)
    A.   Persian Challenge
        1. Darius and Marathon
        2. Xerxes, Thermopylae, and the Victory at Salamis
    B.   Athenian Empire
        1. Organization of the Delian League
        2. Golden Age of Pericles
            a. Democracy Achieved
            b. Athenian Imperialism
    C.   Peloponnesian War (431-404 B.C.)
        1. Thucydides' Story
        2. Plague and the Death of Pericles
        3. Alcibiades Debacle
        4. Spartan Victory
    D.   Decline of the Greek City-States (404-338 B.C.)
        1. Breakup of Coalitions
        2. Philip II and the Rise of Macedonia

V. The Culture and Society of Classical Greece
        1. The Writing of History
            a. Herodotus' *History of the Persian Wars*
            b. Thucydides' *History of the Peloponnesian War*
        2. Greek Drama
            a. Aeschylus and the *Oresteia*
            b. Sophocles and *Oedipus the King*
            c. Euripides and *The Bacchae*
            d. Comedy and Aristophanes
        3. Arts and the Classical Ideal
        4. Philosophy: The Greek Love of Wisdom
            a. Sophists
            b. Socrates
            c. Plato and *The Republic*
            d. Aristotle and *Politics*
        5. Greek Religion
            a. Gods
            b. Panhellenic Festivals at Olympia and Delphi
            c. Mysteries of Demeter
        6. Daily Life in Classical Athens
            a. Slavery
            b. Trade and Crafts
            c. Family Life: Men and Women
            d. Homosexuality

Chapter Summary

Although they borrowed freely from the ancient civilizations of Mesopotamia and Egypt, the Greeks, employing their own genius, created the first distinctively Western civilization. We can see their hand in the fashioning of modern Western languages, philosophy, and art. Theirs was the first truly Western culture.

The Greeks of the Classical age, those whose names and works we most readily recognize, were the product of long years of cultural development. The peoples who inhabited the rough hills of the Hellenic peninsula, the coast of Asia-Minor, and the islands between them worked for many generations to bring about the flowering of civilization that we call the Golden Age of Greece.

On the island of Crete and later on the mainland at Mycenae, early Greeks (who called themselves Hellenes) fashioned the language, thought, and art that would blossom into their finest forms in the fifth and fourth centuries B.C. The Greeks who attacked and fought with Troy around 1250 B.C. were chronicled by Homer around 800 B.C. The city states of Athens and Sparta, leaders in the Classical Age, had been developing their contrasting institutions and life style for three centuries before 500 B.C.

The "archaic" period of Greek history is the prelude to the greatest Greek age. Between the Greek defeat of a Persian invasion force in 479 B.C. and the conquest of the Greek city-states by Philip II of Macedon in 338 B.C., the Greeks produced a civilization that is still today considered a high point in Western history. During this time Greek philosophy, culminating in the works of Socrates, Plato, and Aristotle, asked the questions and provided the answers philosophers still ponder and debate. During this time Greek dramatists, Aeschylus, Sophocles, Euripides, and Aristophanes, created a form of literary art that evolved into modern theater. During this time Greek art and architecture discovered forms so human, so universal, that they are still admired and imitated throughout the Western world and beyond.

Western civilization's languages, thought patterns, and aesthetic values all come directly from the Greeks. Greece is for Western peoples the "mother country".

Learning Objectives

1. Be able to demonstrate how the geography of Greece molded Greek history and the culture it produced.

2. Be able to explain the coming of the Greek "Dark Age" and how it produced the works of Homer.

3. Be able to describe the centerpiece of Greek culture, the *polis*, and show how and why it took such different forms in Sparta and Athens.

4. Be able to list the major themes of classical Greek philosophy, the achievements of the great philosophers, and the ways in which their thought is still alive today.

5. Be able to discuss the Greek ideal of beauty and demonstrate how it found expression in Greek art and architecture.

Glossary of Names and Terms

1. Mycenae: a central city of the early Greek civilization called Mycenaean, characterized by military adventures and conquest, identified by Homer as the home of the warriors who fought Troy.

2. Homer: writer of the eighth century B.C. who recorded oral tales to create the epic Greek classics *Iliad* and *Odyssey*.

3. Solon: Athenian lawgiver who defined a citizen as one who involves himself in public affairs and encouraged more Athenians to participate in government.

4. Sappho: Greek writer of love poems, resident of Lesbos, whose songs often spoke of her attraction to her female pupils.

5. Thermopylae: mountain pass where a Greek army held off an invading Persian force for two days until betrayed, after which the city of Athens had to be abandoned.

6. Aeschylus: earliest of the great Greek tragedians, whose *Oresteia* is the only complete extant example of the Greek trilogy.

7. Aristophanes: the greatest of the Greek comedians, author of *The Clouds* (making fun of philosophers and *Lysistrata* (poking ridicule at warriors).

8. Plato: student of Socrates who in his writings made his teacher the spokesman for his revolutionary thoughts about the nature of reality and the perfect state.

9. Aristotle: student of Plato whose treatises on nature and politics heavily influenced Western thought for many centuries.

10. Orpheus: legendary singer whose followers believed in cycles of reincarnation and sought to free the human soul from physical entrapment.

Match these Words with their Definitions

1. Polis

2. Marathon

3. Pericles

4. Herodotus

5. Thucydides

6. Sophocles

7. Euripides

8. Acropolis

9. Sophist

10. Aristotle

A.   Athenian statesman of the Golden Age

B.   Author of *The Peloponnesian War*

C.   Greek playwright who created *The Bacchae*

D.   Central focus of Greek political, social, and religious life

E.   A Greek wandering teacher who emphasized rhetoric over logic

F.   Greek playwright who chronicled the story of Oedipus

G.   Site of the Athenian victory over the Persians in 490 B.C.

H.   Author of *Ethics* and tutor to Alexander the Great

I.   Sacred site of the Parthenon

J.   The "Father of History" who wrote *The Persian Wars*

Choose the Correct Answer

1.   The greatest statement praising Athenian democracy can be found in

   a.   Sophocles' *Oedipus the King*
   b.   Pericles' *Funeral Oration*
   c.   Aristophanes' *Lysistrata*
   d.   Plato's *Republic*
   e.   Aristotle's *Politics*

2.   The British amateur archeologist Arthur Evans uncovered the

   a.   Delphic Temple
   b.   Palace of Knossus
   c.   Stadium of Olympia
   d.   Mystery Precinct of Eleusis
   e.   Battlefield of Marathon

3.   The epic poems *Iliad* and *Odyssey*

   a.   Reveal the circumstances of early Greek life
   b.   Reflect a society in which the warrior-aristocrat was dominant
   c.   Existed as oral traditions before being written down
   d.   Are less than reliable historical documents
   e.   All of the above

4. The best word to describe the social and political organization of Homeric Greece is

    a. Democratic---rule by the people
    b. Aristocratic---rule by a warrior minority
    c. Plutocratic---rule by wealthy merchants
    d. Theocratic---rule by priests
    e. Dynastic---rule by divinely appointed royal families

5. Tyranny in the Greek *polis* arose as

    a. People became complacent due to the success of democracy
    b. A response to the cry for strong leadership from established aristocratic oligarchies
    c. The power of kings waned in the eighth century B.C.
    d. The religious faith of the Greeks floundered
    e. Hunger drove populations to desperate covenants

6. The poems of Sappho reflect

    a. A strong devotion to morality and personal integrity
    b. An unselfconscious acceptance of homosexual sentiments
    c. An aristocratic disdain for the lower classes
    d. Political musings of a sixth-century politician
    e. Philosophical theories of a budding Platonist

7. Which of the following statements best describes Athens in 500 B.C.?

    a. It was united and primed for its period of greatness
    b. It was the only city-state that had avoided tyranny in Archaic Greece
    c. It was an unlikely setting to be the birthplace of democracy
    d. It had provided equality for all its residents
    e. It was no longer able to provide enough food for its citizens

8. The play that does not illustrate Greek tragedy is

    a. Sophocles' *Oedipus the King*
    b. Aristophanes' *Lysistratra*
    c. Euripides' *The Bacchae*
    d. Aeschylus' *Oresteia*
    e. Aristotle's *Genetics*

9. Which of the following statements is *not* true of classical Greek art?

    a. The temple was the most important form of architecture
    b. Columns in temples were of various styles
    c. Sculpture followed the *kouros* style
    d. Art and architecture followed well-defined laws of proportion
    e. Symmetry, balance, and harmony prevailed

10. Greek classical art emphasized

    a. The beauty of the human form
    b. Ideal forms in its representation of the human form
    c. The civilizing effect of artistic balance and harmony
    d. The central place of religion each city's welfare
    e. All of the above

11. Early Greek philosophy attempted to

    a. Destroy belief in the gods
    b. Undermine traditional Greek values and morals
    c. Explain the universe through unifying principles
    d. Establish a moral code for the lower classes
    e. Demonstrate the virtues of warfare

12. The philosopher Pythagoras said that the universe is best understood through the study of

    a. Hydrodynamics
    b. Math and music
    c. The four basic elements
    d. The acts of the gods
    e. Socratic dialogues

13. The Socratic Method did *not* involve

    a. Consulting authorities from the past
    b. Assuming that knowledge is within the person
    c. Asking questions of his opponents in debate
    d. Demonstrating the foolish assumptions of those opponents
    e. Questioning the authority of established powers

14. Plato's *Republic* departed from tradition Greek thought by asserting that

    a. Homosexuality was socially acceptable
    b. Religion was the basis of the perfect society
    c. Democracy would eventually be the norm
    d. Women could and should be rulers
    e. Just societies are based on balance and harmony

15. Plato argued that the best society would be ruled by

    a. Men of deep religious sensitivity and dedication
    b. Men or women of great wealth
    c. Men of philosophy
    d. Men of the sword
    e. Men of good will

Chapter 3

16. In his *Politics* Aristotle argued that

    a. Aristocracy often becomes anarchy
    b. Monarchy often becomes oligarchy
    c. Constitutionalism offers the best hope of justice
    d. Constitutionalism often brings tyranny
    e. Democracy offers the most happiness to the greatest numbers

17. Greek religion was in every case

    a. Administered by enlightened philosophers
    b. A civic cult
    c. Based on a strict body of doctrine
    d. Monotheistic
    e. The vehicle for teaching ethical behavior

18. Which of the following is true of the Athenian economy?

    a. Slaves provided almost the entire work force
    b. Agriculture was growing less important by the decade
    c. Skilled craftsmen were often unemployed for long periods
    d. Public works projects provided a considerable opportunity for employment
    e. No one ever pulled himself up from poverty to riches

19. Athenian women were

    a. Allowed to own private property
    b. Usually given formal education
    c. Considered legally and socially inferior to men
    d. Prohibited from practicing prostitution
    e. Excluded from participation in religious rituals

20. Greek male homosexuality was *not*

    a. Borrowed from Egypt
    b. Tacitly tolerated
    c. An aristocratic ideal
    d. Between an older man and his young lover
    e. Always between men

Complete the Following Sentences

1. Homer's *Iliad* chronicles the siege of _____ and how the anger of _____ led to social chaos and disaster on the _____.

2. In Sparta the life of males was organized around _____ service, with a boy leaving his mother at age _____ and starting active duty at age _____.

3. In Athens Cleisthenes brought unity by creating _____ tribes and a council of _____, laying the foundations for that city's system of _____.

4. The Peloponnesian League dominated by _____ and the Delian League led by _____ eventually came to blows in the destructive _____ _____.

5. The Golden Age of Athens, named for its leader _____, saw the flowering of its _____ and the expansion of its _____.

6. Thucydides saw politics and war in _____ terms, caused by the activities of _____ _____, not the _____.

7. The greatest single example of Classical Greek architecture is the _____, erected on the _____, a temple to the goddess _____.

8. Socrates was convicted of _____ the _____ of Athens, and his final sentence was _____.

9. Plato's distrust of _____ led him to postulate a more _____ state in his _____.

10. Athenian women were under male guardianship throughout their lives, first a _____, then a _____, and often finally a _____.

Place the Following in Chronological Order and Give Dates

1. The Peloponnesian War   1.

2. Construction of the Parthenon   2.

3. The *Iliad* composed   3.

4. Solon's Athenian reforms   4.

5. The Death of Socrates   5.

6. Height of Mycenaean Civilization   6.

7. Battle of Marathon   7.

Questions for Critical Thought

1. Explain how the geography of Greece helped to create and mold Greek society and how it influenced Greek history.

2. Discuss the importance of the writer Homer for the social and intellectual development of the Greeks. By what Homeric standards did later Greeks judge themselves?

3. Discuss the strengths and weaknesses of the Greek polis system. How did it make the Greeks what they were and keep them from being greater? Compare and contrast the development and characteristics of the two greatest Greek city-states, Athens and Sparta. Show how each became what it was and what each contributed to Greek culture.

4. Discuss the cumulative accomplishments of Solon, Pisistratus, and Cleisthenes. What part did each play in the creation of Athenian democracy? Describe the Athenian democracy and show how it was like and unlike our own form.

5. Discuss the contributions Herodotus and Thucydides made to the development of the science of history.

6. Discuss the contributions of Aeschylus, Sophocles, and Euripides to the development of tragedy. Compare the origins, development, and characteristics of Greek tragedy to those of Greek comedy, using Aristophanes as your example.

7. Discuss the contributions of Plato and Aristotle to the development of Greek philosophy. Explain why they are still today considered the two wellsprings of Western philosophy.

8. Why do we say that Greek civilization is the "fountainhead" of Western civilization?

Analysis of Primary Source Documents

1. Using Hector as your example, describe the ideal Homeric hero and his attitude toward war, fate, and women.

2. Describe the way young Spartan men were trained. Explain how being masters of a slave population that greatly outnumbered them led to such training.

3. With her poetry as your example, show why Sappho is considered the first great woman writer. Explain why her celebration of human sexual love has made her controversial at various times?

4. From the brief account of the Battle of Marathon, what do you judge to be Herodotus' strengths as an historian? How does he capture such detailed events in so few words?

5. In his funeral oration, Pericles clearly articulated the virtues of Athenian democracy. What are they? Are his comments relevant around the world today?

6. After reading Thucydides' description of what happened to Athenians after their defeat in Sicily, compare the treatment of prisoners of war then to the treatment today.

7. Discuss the way the Greek comedian Aristophanes used sex both as a comedic device and as a way of making a social statement.

8. Explain Aristotle's argument that man is meant to live in communities. Explain why you agree or disagree with his thesis.

9. Comparing and contrasting the comments of Xenophon, Aristotle, and Plutarch, sketch a picture of how Greek women of various cities and statuses were expected to live and act.

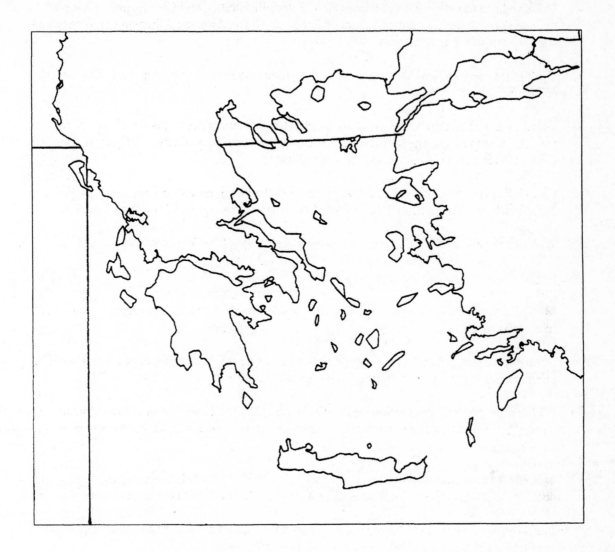

Chapter 3

Map Exercise 2: Greece and the Aegean Basin

Shade and label the following

1. Aegean Sea
2. Asia Minor
3. Attica
4. Crete
5. Delos
6. Gulf of Corinth
7. Hellespont
8. Macedonia
9. Peloponnesus

Pinpoint and label the following

1. Athens
2. Corinth
3. Delphi
4. Marathon
5. Miletus
6. Salamis
7. Sparta
8. Thebes
9. Thermopylae

CHAPTER 4
THE HELLENISTIC WORLD

Chapter Outline

I. Macedonia and the Conquests of Alexander
  A. Philip II and the Conquest of Greece
    1. Demosthenes' Warnings
    2. Philip and the Greek City-States
  B. Alexander the Great
    1. Battle at the Granicus River
    2. Battle of Issus
    3. Ruler of Egypt
    4. Battle of Gaugamela and Conquest of Persia
    5. Alexander's Ideals
    6. Alexander's Legacy

II. World of the Hellenistic Kingdoms
  A. Hellenistic Monarchies
    1. Antigonids of Macedonia
    2. Seleucids of Syria
    3. Ptolemies of Egypt
  B. Threat from the Celts
  C. Political and Military Institutions
    1. Despotism
    2. Rule by Greeks
    3. Warfare
  D. Hellenistic Cities
    1. Greek Culture
    2. Recreation of the *Polis*
  E. Economic Trends
    1. Expanded Economy
    2. New Products

III. Hellenistic Society
  A. New Opportunities for Upper-Class Women
    1. Example of Arsinoë II
    2. Management of Economic Affairs
    3. Education
    4. Arts
  B. Slavery
  C. Education Transformed
    1. Gymnasium
    2. School at Teos

Chapter 4

IV. Culture in the Hellenistic World
    A. Libraries as Centers of Culture
    B. Literature and Art
       1. Theocritus
       2. Menander
       3. Polybius the Historian
       4. Sculpture
    C. Golden Age of Science and Medicine
       1. Aristarchus of Samos
       2. Eratosthenes
       3. Euclid
       4. Archimedes
       5. Hippocrates, Herophilus, and Erasistratus
    D. Philosophy: New Schools of Thought
       1. Epicureanism
       2. Zeno and Stoicism
       3. Problem of Human Happiness

V. Religion in the Hellenistic World
    A. Ruler Cults and Civic Cults
    B. Eastern Cults
    C. Mystery Cults and Personal Salvation
    D. Jews
       1. Maccabaean Revolt
       2. Synagogues

Chapter Summary

The classical age of Greece came to an end, as did native rule in the Persian and Egyptian Empires, with the conquest of the civilized world by Alexander III of Macedonia. Beginning both his reign and his conquests in 336 at the age of 20, ending both his reign and his life in 323 at the age of 32, Alexander dominated the ancient world, only to die at the moment of his highest achievement.

With the life and death of Alexander, an old world died and a new one was born, a world that was Hellenistic or Greek-like, one that combined the essential elements of Greek culture with those of the lands it conquered. It was a world in which all the ancient Mediterranean peoples shared a common yet richly and regionally varied way of life.

During the period from 323 B.C. until the Roman conquest of the Hellenistic world two centuries later, despots of Greek descent ruled various kingdoms that warred sometimes against each other and at other times against outside invaders. The various kings of Syria, Egypt, and Macedonia imitated classical culture with their encouragement of Greek styles in art and architecture as well as schools that taught Greek language and thought. During this age science separated itself from philosophy and became a distinct field of study. Great strides were made in medicine. Euclid invented geometry. Polybius followed in the footsteps of Thucydides in the writing of history. Erastothenes built the famous library in Alexandria. Epicurus and Zeno started new philosophical traditions. Religious cults and mystery religions proved that urban and sophisticated Hellenistic men and women were as hungry for spiritual nourishment as those before and after them.

While it is impossible to imagine the Hellenistic Age without the Hellenic one before it, it is equally impossible to imagine the Roman Age or even the Christian Age that followed without the Hellenistic Age. It was a bridge, but a bridge with a beauty, a character, and a life all its own.

36

Learning Objectives

1. Be able to recount, explain, and show the long term significance of Alexander's conquests.

2. Be able to explain how the Hellenistic system worked, its debts to classical Greece, and its legacy for later history.

3. Be able to describe Hellenistic cities and their role in preserving and extending the Greek ideal.

4. Be able to discuss the economic and social structures of the Hellenistic world, their successes and their shortcomings.

5. Be able to describe the cultural achievements of the Hellenistic Age, particularly its scientific and philosophical contributions to history.

Glossary of Names and Terms

1. Demosthenes: Athenian writer and orator who spurred his city to go to war to oppose the growing power of Philip of Macedon and thereby led to Athens' subjugation.

2. Alexander the Great: son of Philip who continued his father's conquests and eventually created the greatest empire to that time.

3. Hellenism: the political, economic, and cultural system that dominated the known world after the death of Alexander, a bridge between the ages of classical Greece and Rome

4. Menander: Athenian playwright who led the Hellenistic Age in writing New Comedy, abandoning political themes simply to entertain and amuse audiences.

5. Polybius: Greek historian who wrote of the rise of Rome as a great power, following Thucydides' goal of providing logical reasons for historical events.

6. Euclid: Alexandrian mathematician who wrote the standard textbook for the study of plane geometry, a book used into the modern age.

7. Hippocrates: philosopher who made medicine a separate category of learning, searching for natural causes and cures for diseases.

8. Epicurus: Athenian philosopher who taught that happiness is the goal of life and that man should pursue pleasure, the only true good.

9. Zeno: Athenian philosopher whose teachings, Stoicism, stressed the centrality of virtue as the means of achieving human happiness, a philosophy which became the most popular in the Hellenistic and Roman eras.

10. Judas Maccabaeus: Jewish leader who rose in rebellion against the seizure of the temple in Jerusalem by the Hellenistic monarch, an event celebrated now by the festival of Hanukkah.

Chapter 4

Match these Words with their Definitions

1. Demosthenes

2. Chaeronea

3. Gaugamela

4. Roxane

5. Antigonus

6. Seleucus

7. Ptolemy

8. Gymnasiarch

9. Polybus

10. Maccabaeus

A. Alexander's successor in Egypt

B. Jewish leader who led revolt against the Syrian Antiochus IV

C. Hellenistic historian

D. Alexander's successor in Persia and Syria

E. Sit of Alexander's first military command

F. Site near Babylon where Alexander defeated the Persian army

G. Hellenistic educator

H. Bactrian wife of Alexander

I. Alexander's successor in Macedonia

J. Athenian opponent of Philip II

Choose the Correct Answer

1. Prior to the reign of Philip II, the Macedonians

    a. Were admired by other Greeks for their culture
    b. Spoke a Persian dialect unknown to the Greeks
    c. Were a rural people organized into tribal units
    d. Lived in city-states under democracy
    e. Never had a king

2. *The Philippics* were a series of orations in which

    a. Demosthenes called Philip II a savior who would save the Greeks from themselves
    b. Demosthenes tried to convince the Athenians to fight against the treacherous Philip II
    c. Isocrates spurred the Athenian assembly to action against Philip II
    d. Isocrates urged Athens to join Philip II in war
    e. Philip explained his goal of uniting all Greeks

3. Alexander's military success against the Persians was largely attributed to

    a. The chronic weakness of Persian institutions
    b. Greek scientific and medical superiority
    c. The role of Alexander's cavalry
    d. Greek naval superiority
    e. The convincing prophesies of Greek oracles

4. The Hellenistic age saw

    a. The extension of the Greek language and ideas to all the ancient Near East
    b. The absence of autocratic power for nearly three centuries
    c. The disappearance of a Greek cultural legacy
    d. Alexander's successors maintain a united empire
    e. The rise of the new Christian faith

5. Hellenistic cities were

    a. Examples of democratic government at work
    b. Thoroughly lawless and dangerous
    c. Islands of Greek culture in a sea of non-Greeks
    d. Ruled by non-Greek viceroys loyal to Greek kings
    e. Primarily agricultural centers with few cultural amenities

6. Which of the following statements best applies to the status of women in the Hellenistic world?

    a. No advancements were made for women in the economic fields, since it was illegal for women to handle money
    b. In most kingdoms the queen shared equal power with the king, raising the prestige of upper-class women in general
    c. While women in Sparta were strictly supervised, Athenian women were allowed to share in men's affairs
    d. As males were preferred to females, lower-class women were commonly subjected to infanticide or were condemned to lives as prostitutes
    e. Most of the scientific discoveries of the age came from experiments carried out by upper class women

7. Education in the Hellenistic Age was

    a. Dependent on the contributions of rich patrons
    b. Strictly for boys only
    c. Oriented toward science and technology
    d. Supervised by the city-states
    e. Conducted by slaves, often better educated than their masters

8. Menander's New Comedy featured

    a. Complex plots featuring noble aristocrats
    b. Soldiers fighting in Alexander's wars
    c. Simple plots with happy endings
    d. The myths of classical Greece
    e. Explosions using the newly discovered "Greek fire"

9. The surviving works of the Greek historian Polybius demonstrate

    a. That he followed Thucydides in seeking rational motives for historical events
    b. His interest in the growth of the Greek city-states
    c. The failure of ancient historians to find firsthand accounts for their narratives
    d. The obsession of ancient historians with sex
    e. His bias toward the oppressed lower classes over the dominant ruling classes

10. Science in the Hellenistic era

    a. Accepted Aristarchus' heliocentric universe
    b. Concentrated on inventing labor-saving devices
    c. Separated itself from philosophy to become a distinct field
    d. Achieved little in the field of mathematics
    e. First discovered and explained the atom

11. Alexandrian physicians

    a. Made extensive use of amulets and herbal remedies
    b. Pioneered in dissection and vivisection
    c. Had little lasting influence on medical history
    d. Served only members of the royal family
    e. Expounded the first primitive theory of germs

12. The Alexandrian scholar Euclid's most famous achievement was

    a. Developing a theory of epicycles to explain the earth's orbit
    b. His systematization and organization of geometric theories
    c. Formulating and synthesizing the basic principles in military science
    d. Transferring the capital of Hellenistic science from Athens to Alexandria
    e. His book *Elements*, which demonstrated the atomic theory of medicine

13. The most famous scientist of his day, Archimedes, did all of the following *except*

    a. Drew sketches for a submarine and parachute
    b. Designed military devices that were capable of turning back sieges
    c. Perfected the science of hydrostatics
    d. Established the value of the mathematical constant "pi"
    e. Wrote a book on the geometry of spheres and cylinders

14. The philosophy known as Stoicism

    a. Rejected God and lacked a spiritual foundation
    b. Never achieved widespread popularity and essentially died out with its founder Zeno
    c. Regarded a life of public service as noble and virtuous
    d. Rejected equality among humans as a pipe dream
    e. Proved entirely compatible with Judaism

15. The popularity of Stoicism and Epicureanism in the Hellenistic world

    a. Demonstrated the strength of the polis
    b. Came despite the growth of traditional Greek religious practices
    c. Suggested a new openness to the concept of universality
    d. Showed how important sexual matters were to men of the time
    e. Is a myth perpetuated by their few devotees

16. Hellenistic mystery religions were characterized by all of the following *except*

    a. An emphasis on personal salvation
    b. A savior god who brought eternal life
    c. Elaborate and emotional rituals of initiation
    d. A training course of written instructions
    e. A multitude of shrines, making access easy for everyone

17. The Hellenistic Cult of Isis

    a. Came originally from Egypt
    b. Offered hope to women and children
    c. Promised its followers eternal life
    d. Portrayed Isis as the giver of law and literature to mankind
    e. All of the above

18. The mystery cults of the Hellenistic world

    a. Were foreign to classical Greek culture
    b. Helped pave the way for the success of Christianity
    c. Offered the average person little comfort in life
    d. Lacked effective initiation ceremonies
    e. Were popular only in rural areas

19. Seizure of the Temple in Jerusalem in 164 B.C. by a Syrian army led to

    a. The establishment of a new Jewish kingdom
    b. The celebration of the festival of Hanukkah
    c. Destruction of the City of David
    d. A civil war between Jewish factions
    e. The execution of most Jewish priests

20. The Hellenistic Age suffered all but one of these problems

    a. Arrogant foreign rulers
    b. Continuing inconclusive wars
    c. Lack of scientific and philosophical imagination
    d. A wide gulf between rich and poor
    e. Separation of Greek rulers and landlords from native populations

Complete the Following Sentences

1. The decisive battle that allowed Alexander to capture Persia's capitals took place at
   _____, where he defeated the forces of Emperor _____ by the effective use of
   his heavy _____.

2. In order to strengthen ties between Greeks and the people they conquered, Alexander
   encouraged his soldiers to _____ _____ women, as he did with _____ and
   _____.

3. Alexander's successor in Egypt was _____, in Syria _____, and in
   Macedonia _____.

4. Hellenistic armies added to Alexander's traditional _____ and _____ the use
   of _____, the "tank" of the ancient world.

5. In the Hellenistic Age slaves were most often _____ children, persons kidnapped by
   _____, and _____ of _____.

6. The gymnasiarch in the Hellenistic era headed the _____ system of his city
   without _____, but he was often given a _____ _____ in appreciation for his
   services.

7. The most famous Hellenistic library, located in _____, boasted some _____
   scrolls and encouraged _____ studies of language and literature.

8. Polybus wrote _____ books detailing the history of the _____ world, with special
   emphasis on the rise of_____.

9. During the Hellenistic era the field of _____ broke away from _____ to
   become a discipline of its own. It then made great discoveries in the fields of _____
   and _____.

10. The school of philosophy that stressed the attainment of happiness through freeing oneself
    from public and political life was _____, while Zeno's rival philosophy,
    _____, emphasized the universal brotherhood of man.

Place the Following in Chronological Order and Give Dates

1. Birth of Polybius   1.

2. Death of Alexander III   2.

3. Death of Epicurus   3.

4. Uprising led by Judas Maccabaeus   4.

5. Reign of Philip II   5.

6. Battle of Gaugamela   6.

7. Battle of Issus   7.

Questions for Critical Thought

1. Describe the way Alexander the Great "liberated" the countries he conquered. Of what practical value was his habit of taking for himself the titles of leaders he deposed?

2. What were Alexander's goals; and what legacy did he leave behind? How close did his legacy come to matching his goals?

3. Describe the typical Hellenistic city, and show how it transmitted Greek culture to the people within and around it.

4. Explain how and why women's lot improved during the Hellenistic age. What were the long-term results of this improvement?

5. Explain the reasons for and results of the great transformation in education that occurred in the Hellenistic age.

6. Historians agree that the Hellenistic age was a time of unusual scientific achievement. Explain how and why this is true.

7. Compare and contrast the two great philosophies developed during the Hellenistic era, Epicureanism and Stoicism. What particular needs did they serve, and how successful were they in meeting those needs?

8. Explain how the Jewish people responded and adapted to Hellenism. What gave them their unique perspective and motivation?

Chapter 4

Analysis of Primary Source Documents

1. Why did Demosthenes oppose the rise of Philip II? Why did Isocrates welcome it? How do their very different speeches reflect the ambivalent attitude of Athenians toward this foreigner?

2. Why did Alexander admire the Indian Porus? How did he show this admiration? What military "code" did he demonstrate?

3. What do the two letters tell us about the status and social roles of Hellenistic women? Explain the contradictions.

4. Describe the life of a slave in Hellenistic Egypt's mines. How did it differ from the life of a slave in classical Athens? What accounts for such a difference?

5. Although little is known about the life of Hellenistic poet Theocritus, what can you tell of his interests and values from his *Seventh Idyll*?

6. Discuss the cures attributed to Asclepius at his shrine in Epidaurus. How would a modern scientist explain such miracles?

7. Recount as many principles of Stoicism as you can find in Cleanthes' *Hymn to Zeus*. To what social class did his ideals appeal? Explain.

CHAPTER 5
THE ROMAN REPUBLIC

Chapter Outline

I. Emergence of Rome
    A. Geography of the Italian Peninsula
    B. Greek Influences
    C. Etruscan Influences
    D. Early Rome (to 509 B.C.)
        1. Legend of Romulus and Remus
        2. Etruscan Domination
        3. Freedom from the Etruscans

II. Roman Republic (509-264 B.C.)
    A. Roman State
        1. Political Institutions
            a. Senate
            b. Assembly
        2. Social Organizations
            a. Paterfamilias
            b. Names
            c. Patricians and Plebians
            d. Struggle of the Orders
    B. Roman Conquest of Italy
        1. Leader of Latium
        2. Livy's Stories

III. Roman Conquest of the Mediterranean (264-133 B.C.)
    A. Struggle with Carthage
        1. First Punic War
        2. Second Punic War
            a. Hannibal
            b. Fabius the Delayer
            c. Scipio Africanus
        3. Third Punic War
    B. Eastern Mediterranean
    C. Roman Imperialism
    D. Evolution of the Roman Army

IV. Society and Culture in the Roman Republic
    A. Religion
        1. Greek Influences
        2. Rituals and Pontiffs
        3. Augurs and Omens
        4. Household Cults
        5. Festivals

B. Education
    1. Family Training
    2. Rhetoric for Public Life
    3. The Importance of the Greek Language
C. Slavery
    1. Uses of Slaves
    2. Treatment
D. Family
    1. *Paterfamilias*
    2. Women
E. Law
    1. Twelve Tables
    2. Law of Nations
F. Literature and Art
    1. Plautus
    2. Terence
    3. Cato the Elder
    4. Arch
    5. The Arch
    6. Statuary
G. Values and Attitudes

V. Decline and Fall of the Roman Republic (133-31 B.C.)
A. Social, Economic, and Political Problems
    1. Rule by *Nobiles*
    2. Division of the Aristocrats
    3. Role of Equestrians
    4. Land Problems
B. Reforms of Tiberius and Gaius Gracchus
C. Marius and the New Roman Army
D. The Role of Sulla
E. Death of the Republic
    1. Pompey
    2. Cicero
    3. Pompey and Caesar
    4. Antony and Cleopatra
    5. Octavian and Antony
F. Literature in the Late Republic
    1. Catullus' Lyric Poetry
    2. Lucretius' Epicurean Verse
    3. Cicero's Orations
    4. Sallust's Histories
    5. Julius Caesar's *Commentaries*

Chapter Summary

Among the half dozen most important cities of Western civilization is Rome. Rome was the nucleus of the Roman Empire, served as its capital and center of culture, and today still haunts the memory of Western man.

At first only one among many small towns founded on the Latin Plain in the eighth century B.C., Rome was strongly influenced in its early days by Greek colonials and Etruscan overlords. After gaining its independence, however, it came to dominate first the Latin Plain, then all of Italy, and finally the whole Mediterranean world. Through a series of wars, first with western rival Carthage and then with eastern rival Macedonia, Rome mastered and was in turn mastered by the civilizations of the ancient Near East and Greece. For over 600 years a city able to conquer militarily and willing to be conquered culturally by its vanquished rivals ruled the Western world.

With a system of government and laws born of its paternal social structure, Rome adapted its institutions to the demands of empire. As its military and political authority spread across land and sea, its early republicanism gave way to civilian and then military dictatorships, and finally to men who bore the title emperor. While the first Roman with truly imperial ambitions, Julius Caesar, was assassinated by a band of jealous senators, his nephew and successor Octavian became in fact the first Roman emperor. With the accession of this "August One" to power, republican Rome gave way with both a sigh and a raised fist to imperial Rome, which would guide civilization for half a millennium.

The Roman Republic produced literary figures such as the playwright Plautus and orator Cicero, but it also produced the reformers Tiberius and Gaius Gracchus. The republic's Julius Caesar was both a military conqueror and a writer of distinction. This was the time when the Rome of grandeur was born.

Learning Objectives

1.	Be able to recount the early development of the Roman people prior to the creation of the Roman Republic.

2.	Be able to describe the social and political institutions of early Rome and the consequences of the struggle of the orders.

3.	Be able to explain why and how Rome came to dominate the Italian peninsula and then the entire Mediterranean world.

4.	Be able to discuss the major characteristics of Roman Republican culture and explain how they were both borrowed from and expanded to meet the needs of conquered peoples.

5.	Be able to explain why the Roman Republic declined and was eventually replaced by the Roman Empire.

Glossary of Names and Terms

1. Lucretia: the literary and mythical model of the Roman woman, faithful, pure, and courageous, who after being raped committed suicide rather than be an unchaste wife.

2. *Paterfamilias*: head of the Roman household who served as a miniature head of state for his family, which formed a tight social unit.

3. *Plebiscita*: a measure adopted by the popular assembly, which was composed of the lower classes (plebians) and legally binding only on them, not on the Patricians.

4. Hannibal: ruler of Carthage who invaded Italy in the third century B.C. and threatened Rome but was eventually defeated by Scipio, opening the way for Roman conquest of the western Mediterranean.

5. Cato: conservative Roman senator whose constant call for the complete destruction of Carthage led to the third and decisive war between the two cities.

6. Augurs: a college of Roman men assigned the task of interpreting signs or warnings from the gods, without whose approval the Roman army would not fight.

7. Terence: one of the major Roman playwrights whose work transcended slapstick to achieve artistic expression and subtle character study.

8. Gracchi: Roman brothers whose attempts at economic reform and violent deaths demonstrated the crisis the Republic faced in the second century B.C.

9. Cicero: orator and writer who analyzed the Roman Republic's crisis and called for a "concord of the orders."

10. Caesar: military hero who rose to supreme power in Rome only to be assassinated by members of the Senate in 44 B.C.

Match these Words with their Definitions

1. Latium

2. Livy

3. *Cognomen*

4. Fabius

5. Corinth

6. Pontiffs

7. *Latifundia*

8. First Triumvirate

9. Second Triumvirate

10. Actium

A. Leader of a revolt that made Greece a Roman province

B. Roman officials who oversaw state religious rituals

C. The alliance that included Julius Caesar

D. The geographical area in which Rome is located

E. Roman estates often tended by slaves

F. Descriptive title that could become hereditary

G. Roman general who won by delaying battles

H. Historian whose books give valuable but at time mythical information about early Rome

I. Site of the battle that sealed Antony's doom

J. The alliance that included Octavian

Choose the Correct Answer

1. The Greeks directly influenced the early Romans in all these fields *except*

    a. The cultivation of the olive and vine
    b. The use of a phonetic alphabet
    c. Law and social order
    d. Architectural style
    e. Literary styles and subject matter

2. It is probable that the Etruscans gave to the Romans all of the following *except*

    a. Skill in the use of iron
    b. The symbol of the *fasces*
    c. The alphabet, which they learned from the Greeks
    d. Styles in clothing
    e. A deep suspicion of monarchy

3. The term *imperium* referred to the

    a. Symbol of prosperity seen in Roman art
    b. Right of the family's oldest son to succeed his father
    c. Right of a Roman official to command
    d. Length of an elected official's term of office
    e. Borders of the Roman state

4. Which of the following resulted from the struggle between the plebeian and the patrician orders?

    a. For the first time intermarriage between the orders was legal
    b. Laws passed by the plebian assembly were binding on all Romans
    c. Rome became a democracy
    d. The Senate had the right to pass on all legislation
    e. The Roman army was placed under the command of one official

5. The senatorial aristocracy called *nobiles* was composed
    a. Exclusively of patricians
    b. Exclusively of plebians
    c. Of wealthy patricians or plebians
    d. Of military leaders who had distinguished themselves in battle
    e. Of men who had distinguished themselves in literature or art

6. The significance of Scipio Africanus during the Second Punic War was that he

    a. Impeded Hannibal's advance into Italy through delaying tactics
    b. Won the decisive Battle of Zama
    c. Negotiated a valuable alliance with the Gauls against Hannibal
    d. First used elephants as "living tanks"
    e. Persuaded Rome to destroy the city of Carthage

7. The Roman senator Cato

    a. Proposed an alliance with Carthage
    b. Proposed an alliance with other Africans empires against Carthage
    c. Called for the total destruction of Carthage
    d. Called for a benign neglect of Carthaginian demands
    e. Led an army into Africa against Hannibal

8. Roman officials called "pontiffs" were in charge of

    a. Maintaining proper relations between the state and the gods
    b. Building the infrastructure that enabled Rome to conquer the world
    c. Planning military campaigns
    d. Negotiating treaties with foreign powers
    e. Interpreting signs and omens

9. The core of the upper class Roman educational curriculum

    a. Rhetoric and philosophy
    b. Mathematics and engineering
    c. Military training and physical enhancement
    d. Music and art
    e. Literature and architecture

10. In 73 A.D. a rebellion shook Rome, led by Spartacus, who was a

    a. Soldier from Persia
    b. Merchant from Egypt
    c. Gladiator from Thrace
    d. Religious prophet from Palestine
    e. Senator from a family in political decline

11. The Roman playwright Terence

    a. Married into the Roman royal family
    b. Was exiled for writing pornography
    c. Was freed from slavery by a Roman senator
    d. Died in the Third Punic War
    e. Lived to see over a hundred of his plays produced

12. Which of the following is *not* true of Roman values and beliefs before the creation of the empire?

    a. One must closely follow the customs of one's ancestors
    b. One must show deep respect for parental authority
    c. One must put duty before personal gain
    d. One must trust one's own judgment concerning the will of the gods
    e. One must follow the rules set down by religious authorities

13. The reforms of Gaius and Tiberius Gracchus

    a. Created a system of absolute senatorial power
    b. Eliminated the position of Tribune of the Plebeians
    c. Resulted in further instability and violence as they polarized social groups
    d. Were a complete success, bringing democratic reforms
    e. Eliminated all patrician power in domestic affairs

14. As a reward for their work in the reform movement, the Gracchus brothers

    a. Spent a comfortable retirement on a land grant in Spain
    b. Were made consuls for life
    c. Both died violently
    d. Were financially ruined and died in poverty
    e. Are now considered the greatest of Roman leaders

15. Marius was an unusual consul because he was a

    a. Recently retired military officer
    b. Non-believer who rejected traditional Roman religious practices
    c. *Novus homo* from the equestrian order
    d. Known deviate who practiced unusual sexual rituals
    e. Greek who had risen from slavery

16. The importance of Sulla to Roman history was that he was the

    a. First Roman consul born in the Far East
    b. First Roman general to use siege engines
    c. Diplomat who arbitrated the dispute between Pompey and Caesar
    d. General who restored the senate to power and then voluntarily retired
    e. General who proved that military power alone could not give a man power

17. Julius Caesar

    a. Defeated Crassus at the Battle of Pharsalus in 48 B.C.
    b. Began the Romanization of Gaul and Spain
    c. Dissolved the Senate when he became dictator for life
    d. Was assassinated because he was such a strong republican
    e. Voluntarily relinquished power because of his epilepsy

18. Leading senators sought to end the conflict between Pompey and Caesar by

    a. Proposing that Caesar lay down his command and return to Rome as a private citizen
    b. Proposing that Caesar rule and Pompey be his viceroy
    c. Plotting the assassination of Pompey when he returned from Spain
    d. Plotting the assassination of Caesar when he returned from Egypt
    e. Stripping both men of their military commands

19. The Second Triumvirate ended finally when

    a. Julius Caesar was assassinated
    b. Octavian threw his support to Lepidus against Antony
    c. Marc Antony committed suicide in Egypt
    d. Caesar's son by Cleopatra died at Roman hands
    e. Octavian died at Actium

20. All of the following were true of literature in the late republic *except* that

    a. Octavian celebrated the deeds of his famous uncle Julius in an epic poem
    b. Lucretius followed the Greek pattern of teaching philosophy through poetry
    c. Cicero reached the apex of classical learning in his orations and commentaries
    d. Sallust's histories searched for moral lessons in human events
    e. Caesar's commentaries reached high literary levels while advancing his career

Complete the Following Sentences

1. Rome was built on _____ hills overlooking the plain of _____ on the _____ River.

2. The Etruscan *fasces*, an _____ surrounded by a bundle of _____, became a Roman symbol of _____.

3. In Roman society the male head of a family was called _____, and related families were grouped into clans called _____.

4. The Hortensian Law said that decisions made by the _____ assembly were binding on all Romans, whether _____ or _____.

5. Quintius Fabius held Hannibal at bay in Italy by his tactic of _____ confrontation, while Scipio later invaded _____ _____ and defeated Hannibal.

6. In the east Rome at first defended the _____ states against control by _____; but after a revolt led by _____ Rome itself subdued and controlled them.

7. Roman pontiffs had authority over the _____ ____, maintaining the right relationship between the _____ and the _____.

8. Because the core of Roman education was _____ literature, educated Romans were all _____.

9. Plautus borrowed his _____ and the use of _____ and _____ characters from Greek New Comedy.

10. The Romans used the arch in constructing their _____ and _____; for building material they often used _____.

Place the Following in Chronological Order and Give Dates

1. First Macedonian War   1.

2. Consulships of Marius   2.

3. Octavian defeats Antony   3.

4. Creation of the Roman Confederation   4.

5. Publication of the Twelve Tables   5.

6. Assassination of Julius Caesar   6.

7. First Punic War   7.

Questions for Critical Thought

1. Discuss the characteristics of Roman society which enabled it to grow from a small city to an empire.

2. How did the Etruscans and Greeks influence the early development of Rome's culture and politics? What Etruscan and Greek characteristics did the Roman Republic exhibit?

3. Describe the Roman class system, and show how struggles between the different groups led to Rome's distinctive political system.

4. Discuss the causes and results of the Punic Wars between Rome and Carthage. How did they help bring about the Roman Empire?

5. Describe the nature of and characteristics of Roman religion. How did it grow out of the Roman experience, and how did it help Rome to become great?

6. Describe the Roman family. Show how it proved an aid to Roman stability and conquest.

7. Point out the major interests and concerns of literature in the Roman Republic. What forms did its writers use to express their concerns?

8. Discuss the reasons the Roman republic declined and fell. Show how and why the republic became an empire. Why did Romans continue to mourn its passing?

Analysis of Primary Source Documents

1. After reading the six excerpts from early Roman law, what principles do you see underlying the Roman legal system? What do these principles tell you about Roman society?

2. Using Livy's account of Cincinnatus, describe the Roman ideal of the patriotic citizen-leader. How did such ideals, portrayed in morality tales, contribute to Rome's successes?

3. Describe the Roman destruction of Carthage, and show what moral lessons some Romans drew from it.

4. What does the description of life for a Vestal Virgin tell you about Rome's emphasis on the proper devotion to religious tradition? To what degree were Romans superstitious? What advantages and what disadvantages do you see in a woman becoming a Vestal Virgin?

5. If we suppose Cato the Elder spoke for Roman males, what can you conclude about their attitude toward women? Did this attitude make Rome stronger or weaker than it would have been with different attitudes?

6. Using the brief excerpt from Plautus' play *Swaggering Soldier*, describe the Roman sense of humor. How would an audience of your contemporaries respond to such humor?

7. According to Sallust, why did the Roman Republic decline and fall? Do you see any of those same signs of trouble in modern republics?

8. Describe the assassination of Julius Caesar, and show how Plutarch's story might be used with dramatic effect by a playwright centuries later.

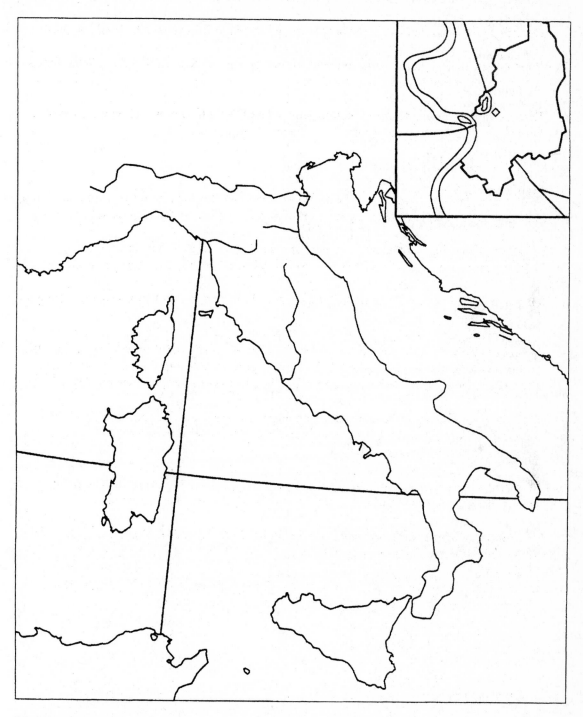

Map Exercise 3

Map Exercise 3: Ancient Italy and the City of Rome

Shade and label the following

1. Adriatic Sea
2. Alps
3. Apennines
4. Corsica
5. Latium
6. Magna Graecia
7. Sardinia
8. Sicily
9. Tyrrhenian Sea

Pinpoint and label the following

1. Arno River
2. Carthage
3. Naples
4. Po River
5. Rome
6. Syracuse
7. Tiber River

(Inset)

8. Appian Way
9. Capitoline Hill
10. Forum

Chapter 6
The Roman Empire

Chapter Outline

I. The Age of Augustus (31 B.C.-A.D. 14)
    A. The New Order
    B. Army
        1. Upward Mobility
        2. Praetorian Guard
        3. *Imperator*
    C. Provinces and Frontiers
        1. Governors
        2. Local Elites
        3. Limits to Expansion
    D. Augustan Society
        1. Senatorial and Equestrian Classes
        2. Lower Classes
        3. Augustus' Reforms
    E. Golden Age of Latin Literature
        1. Virgil's *Aeneid*
        2. Horace's *Satires*
        3. Ovid's *Art of Love*
        4. Livy's *History of Rome*
    F. Significance of the Augustan Age

II. The Early Empire (14-180)
    A. The Julio-Claudians: Tiberius, Caligula, Claudius, and Nero (14-69)
    B. The Flavians: Vespasian, Titus and Domitian (69-96)
    C. The Five "Good Emperors": Nerva, Trajan, Hadrian, Antonius Pius, and Marcus Aurelius (96-180)
    D. Empire at its Height
        1. Frontiers Consolidated
        2. Provinces Strengthened
        3. Use of the Army to Fortify and Romanize
        4. Cities and Romanization
        5. Law and Romanization
    E. Prosperity in the Early Empire
        1. Manufacturing
        2. Trade: Silk Road
        3. Agriculture

Chapter 6

III. Roman Culture and Society in the Early Empire
    1. Silver Age of Latin Literature
       a. Seneca
       b. Petronius
       c. Tacitus
       d. Juvenal
    2. Art and Architecture
    3. Imperial Rome
    4. Gladiatorial Shows
    5. Disaster in Southern Italy
    6. Art of Medicine
    7. Slaves and Masters
    8. Upper-Class Families

IV. Transformation of the Roman World: Crises in the Third Century
    A. Political and Military Woes: Commodus and the Severans (180-235)
    B. Anarchy and Civil War (235-284)
    C. Invasions
    D. Economic and Social Crises

V. Transformation of the Roman World: Development of Christianity
    A. Religious World of the Empire
       1. Official Roman Religion
       2. Mystery Cults
    B. Jewish Background
    C. The Origins of Christianity
       1. Jesus of Nazareth
       2. Paul of Tarsus—Second Founder
       3. Spread of Christianity: Gospels
       4. Early Christian Communities: Eucharist
       5. Changing Roman View of Christianity
       6. Persecution and Martyrs
    D. The Growth of Christianity: Bishops
       1. Christianity and Greco-Roman Culture
       2. Appeal of Christianity
         a. Promise of Salvation
         b. Appeal to All Classes
         c. Women and Early Christianity
         d. Persecution

Chapter Summary

The Roman Empire stands as the strong forbear of Western civilization. It began with the rule of Augustus Caesar and ended five hundred years later in the West with the deposition of Romulus Augustus by barbarians. (It lasted, in diminished size and influence, another thousand years in the East.) It left an indelible impression on the Western world.

Augustus not only centralized the rule of the empire, he helped inaugurate the Golden Age of Roman culture. Under Augustus the Roman Empire functioned smoothly and efficiently, so much so that it survived the series of weak rulers that succeeded him. Augustus instituted a period of peace that lasted for nearly two centuries. Under the influence and inspiration of Augustus, the epic poet Virgil, the rural moralist Horace, the love poet Ovid, and the historian Livy made the Augustan Age one of the high points in human civilization.

Following the reign of Augustus, Rome survived bad emperors and flourished under good ones until the end of the second century, expanding, building, creating a world order never before known. After another century of struggle, it went on adjusting and adapting to change until at long last it gave way to the Middle Ages. As it attempted to fulfill its role as guardian of order, it was at first challenged and later supported by a religion that grew up among but later supplanted the myriad collection of Roman religions—Christianity.

Founded by a Palestinian Jew named Jesus, refashioned into a faith with a universal message by Paul of Tarsus, Christianity offered the people of Rome a unique combination of intellectual and emotional certainty at a time when the world order was threatened by pressures of all kinds. It was only a matter of time, as Rome tottered toward collapse, before Christianity stepped up to offer Western man a new certainty and direction. With the fall of Rome, a new age was born in Western Europe.

Learning Objectives

1. Be able to describe how the empire established by Augustus Caesar worked so well and why it survived for so long after his reign.

2. Be able to describe what the writers of the Golden Age of Latin Literature---Virgil, Horace, Ovid, and Livy---contributed to Roman culture.

3. Be able to name and describe the emperors who succeeded Augustus, how they were chosen, and how they changed the nature of the empire.

4. Be able to detail the various crises that faced the Roman Empire in the third century and show what Roman leaders did and did not to solve the problems they posed.

5. Be able to discuss the rise and growth of the Christian religion and explain how it succeeded against official opposition and persecution.

Glossary of Names and Terms

1. *Princeps*: the title Octavian preferred over Augustus, to be called "first among equals" instead of "revered one."

2. Ovid: last great poet of the Golden Age of Latin Literature, author of *Metamorphoses*, on mythology, and *The Art of Love*.

3. Livy: greatest historian of the early empire, who believed that the study of history provided examples of good and bad behavior, of how to succeed and how not to fail.

4. Nero: only sixteen when he became emperor, he preferred the arts to government and military direction and brought the downfall of the Julio-Claudian line.

5. Seneca: Stoic philosopher of the Silver Age, tutor and assistant to Nero, who amassed a fortune while advocating a simple life.

6. Tacitus: greatest historian of the Silver Age, whose works readily recounted the "evil deeds of wicked men" and who provided the first study of German society.

7. Galen: medical attendant to gladiators who rose to be the personal physician to the emperor Marcus Aurelius and wrote a famous book on human anatomy and disease.

8. Ulpian: jurist who proclaimed that natural law implied that all men are born equal and therefore should be treated with equality before state courts.

9. Essenes: a Jewish sect who lived near the Dead Sea, looked forward to the arrival of the promised messiah, and may have influenced the early Christians.

10. Eucharist: the Christian communal ritual, also called the Lord's Supper, which became the centerpiece of worship, done in memory of the sacrifice of Christ.

Match these Words with their Definitions

1. *Aeneid*

2. *Satires*

3. Trajan

4. Hadrian

5. Marcus Aurelius

6. Pompeii

7. Sadducees

8. Messiah

9. Paul of Tarsus

10. Mithraism

A. Emperor (117-138) who built a wall across Britain

B. Promised One who would come to save Israel

C. Emperor (161-180) who wrote the Stoic classic *Meditations*

D. Precursor to Christianity, featuring a savior-god

E. Considered the "second founder" of Christianity

F. City on the Bay of Naples buried by an eruption from Vesuvius

G. Horace's poems on Roman foibles and vices

H. Hebrew sect that rejected the idea of personal immortality

I. Virgil's epic of the founding of Rome

J. Emperor (284-305) who divided the empire east from west

Choose the Correct Answer

1. The absolute power Augustus held as *princeps* led to

    a. The inevitable victory of his candidates in elections
    b. A decline in popular participation in elections
    c. A decline in the power of popular assemblies
    d. His great personal popularity
    e. All of the above

2. Under Augustus' rule, the Roman Empire

    a. Was a principate in which the Senate ruled for the king
    b. Returned to traditional republican institutions
    c. Turned ever more toward absolute monarchy
    d. Experienced civil war
    e. Adopted Christianity as the state religion

3. Under Augustus the senatorial order

    a. Lost all political power
    b. Ruled as equal partners of the *princeps*
    c. Governed the provinces
    d. Merged with the equestrian order
    e. Adjourned forever

4. Which of the following statements was true of Augustan society?

    a. Popular assemblies of the lower classes grew in power
    b. Legislation was passed to control morals
    c. Equestrians gained the upper hand in politics
    d. Religious observances went into decline
    e. The esteem in which women had once been held declined

5. Virgil's *Aeneid*

    a. Led to his exile from Rome
    b. Included many satirical attacks on human weaknesses
    c. Romanticized the rural life
    d. Connected Roman history and civilization to Greece
    e. Severely criticized corrupt office holders

6. The historian Livy believed that

    a. Morals are irrelevant to a military society
    b. Philosophers should guide politicians in decision making
    c. Human character determines historical developments
    d. History is created from myth
    e. Rome would soon fall because its frontiers were overly extended

7. One or another of the five "good emperors" did all of the following *except*

    a.   Reduced the power and authority of imperial officials
    b.   Carefully controlled who could become a Roman citizen
    c.   Improved harbors and roads in order to bring the empire closer together
    d.   Supported massive building programs throughout the empire
    e.   Established state supported schools for children of poor people

8. Marcus Aurelius is seen as a Platonic figure because he

    a.   Made Athens the empire's cultural center
    b.   Ruled as a philosopher-king
    c.   Built a temple to Socrates in Rome
    d.   Translated the Platonic dialogues into Latin
    e.   Refused to marry so that he could devote his entire life to his rule

9. By the second century Rome's frontier legions were

    a.   Entirely of Italian birth and training
    b.   Entirely non-Italians
    c.   Important instruments for "Romanizing" the provinces
    d.   Constantly pushing back the frontiers of the empire
    e.   Constantly on the defensive against invading German tribes

10. The historian Tacitus sought to

    a.   Recount the history of Rome from Tiberius through Domitian
    b.   Demonstrate the moral lessons of history
    c.   Condemn evil deeds of past generations
    d.   Ensure that merit be recorded for posterity
    e.   All of the above

11. Roman most important contribution to architecture was the use of

    a.   Concrete on a massive scale
    b.   Post and lintel style in temples
    c.   Colonnades to decorate public buildings
    d.   Iron foundations for city walls
    e.   Murals to tell the stories of brave deeds

12. The jurist Ulpian formulated the principles behind the legal concept of

    a.   *Habeas Corpus* or the right to a speedy trial
    b.   Equality of all before the law
    c.   Capital punishment for capital crimes
    d.   Appeals from lower to higher courts
    e.   *Nolo contendre* or the plea of no contest without admitting guilt

13. Medicine in the early Roman Empire was typified by

    a. Galen's attempt to find a cure for baldness and wrinkles
    b. Alcon's dedication to general practice
    c. The establishment of public hospitals in the provinces
    d. The refusal of doctors to treat gladiators
    e. Four year training courses for physicians

14. The "terrible third century" was made so by all of the following *except*

    a. The legalization of Christianity
    b. Civil wars and Germanic invasions
    c. A series of natural disasters and diseases
    d. Serious inflation and a devaluation of coinage
    e. Marcus Aurelius' decision to make his son his successor

15. By the mid-third century Rome's

    a. Official religion was Christianity
    b. Army was composed mostly of hired barbarians
    c. Historians were all predicted catastrophe
    d. Writers were all living in exile
    e. Frontiers had shrunk significantly

16. Which of the following statements does *not* apply to religion in the Roman Empire before the victory of Christianity?

    a. Imperial officials were intolerant of new or foreign religions
    b. The Imperial cults of Roma and Augustus bolstered support for the emperor
    c. Mystery cults such as Mithraism were widely popular
    d. Judaism was divided into various competing sects
    e. Romans considered Christianity a Jewish sect

17. The Jewish monastic group called Essenes

    a. Led an insurrection against Rome in 66 A.D.
    b. Sent missionaries to several Roman provinces
    c. Eventually merged with the Christian Church
    d. Wrote what we call the Dead Sea Scrolls
    e. Emerged from the Jewish diaspora in Spain

18. The growth of Christianity from the second through the fourth centuries can *not* be attributed to its

    a. Efficient organization under bishops
    b. Promise of personal salvation for believers
    c. Appeal both to the mind and the emotions
    d. Involvement in political affairs
    e. Historical founder Jesus of Nazareth

18. Perpetua became a vivid symbol for women who

    a.   Refused to forsake the traditional Roman religions for Christianity
    b.   Died in defense of their falsely accused husbands
    c.   Died rather than forsake their new Christian faith
    d.   Went into battle against the barbarian invaders
    e.   Abandoned a normal married life to be Vestal Virgins

20. The Roman Emperor Decius

    a.   Was the first to become a Christian
    b.   Blamed the Christians for the disasters befalling the empire
    c.   Banned persecutions of any religious group
    d.   Used educated Christians in his imperial administration
    e.   Was a symbol to Christians of a man who died for cursing God

Complete the Following Sentences

1. Augustus Caesar's military exploits were recorded in his _____ _____, which were inscribed on a _____ _____ in Rome.

2. While Augustus never claimed to be a god, he permitted temples to be built to his adoptive father, _____ _____, and encouraged the imperial cult of _____ and _____.

3. Ovid's handbook for seduction, ____ _____ ___ _____, explicitly challenged Augustus' goal of reforming _____ practices among _____ _____ Romans.

4. Livy saw history as _____ _____ and argued that it is the best _____ for a _____ mind.

5. While Rome was the early empire's largest city, _____ in Egypt, _____ in Asia-Minor, and _____ in Syria were also major urban centers.

6. The luxurious life style of the Roman upper class was reflected in the letters of _____ ___ _____ about summer days at one of his rural _____, where he read speeches to aid his _____.

7. Seneca taught that man should accept events as part of the _____ _____; love all of _____; and above all live _____.

8. Gladiatorial shows, held in such amphitheaters as Vespasian's _____, prove that an important part of Roman culture was _____ _____.

9. The Greek Galen was a _____ _____ who rose to be _____ _____ to Marcus Aurelius.

10. Paul, a Jewish Roman citizen born in _____, is said to have given Christianity the _____ _____ it needed to become a major religion.

Place the Following in Chronological Order and Give Dates

1.   Eruption of Mount Vesuvius   1.

2.   Reign of Marcus Aurelius   2.

3.   Persecutions of Decius   3.

4.   Year of the Four Emperors   4.

5.   Jesus' Sermon on the Mount   5.

6.   Death of Augustus   6.

7.   Jewish revolt crushed by Romans   7.

Questions for Critical Thought

1.   Discuss the way Augustus Caesar ruled his new empire, particularly how he organized his government and used his army. How did his policies assure the empire's long-term survival?

2.   Describe the society Augustus created. Why and how did he reform its morals?

3.   What were the major interests and concerns of the writers of Rome's Augustan Age? What literary forms did they employ? Why is this called Rome's Golden Age?

4.   What did the "five good emperors" contribute to the development of the Roman Empire? Why were their policies not effectively continued after them?

5.   Why is the third century labeled by historians a time of crises? Discuss the historical events and human errors and the resulting chaos that made it so bad.

6.   What was the significance of Paul of Tarsus for the development of the Christian faith? Why is he called the "second founder" of Christianity?

7.   How was Christianity able to survive the persecutions it faced in its first three centuries and emerge as the first choice of so many religious Romans? What characteristics made it so attractive to so many people?

8.   What caused Decius to authorize the first systematic persecution of Christians? What does the term "a state within a state" mean?

Analysis of Primary Source Documents

1. Show how the famous inscription *Res Gestae*, the achievements of Augustus, is both history and propaganda.

2. Explain Ovid's theories about "the art of love" and why the moralistic Augustus found them offensive.

3. Describe the Roman Empire at the start of the Year of the Four Emperors. Why would people be willing to accept dictatorship after that year?

4. How did the wealthy Roman spend his leisure time? Why did some commentators later see this lifestyle as one cause of the empire's decline?

5. What does the account by Pliny the Younger about his uncle's death tell you about Roman curiosity and courage? Does Pliny make any judgement about his uncle's wisdom in going to Vesuvius?

6. Describe the incident in 61 A.D. that led to widespread Roman fear of slave rebellions. Why did Romans find the event so surprising and perplexing?

7. Pretend you have just read the Sermon on the Mount by the obscure Jewish teacher, Jesus of Nazareth, for the first time. What would be your estimate of the man who spoke these words?

8. Describe the official state opinion of Christianity in the day of the Emperor Trajan. Then describe the popular pagan accusations against the faith. Why did both officials and the general public think this new religion posed a threat to the Roman state?

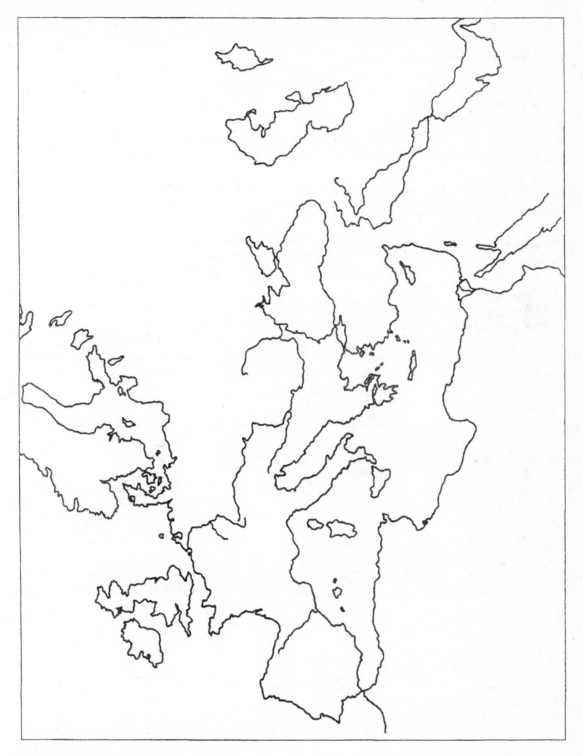

Map Exercise 4

Map Exercise 4: The Roman Empire

Shade and label the following

1. Baltic Sea
2. Black Sea
3. Britain
4. Dacia
5. Egypt
6. Gaul
7. Greece
8. Spain

Pinpoint and label the following

1. Alexandria
2. Constantinople
3. Danube River
4. Jerusalem
5. Ravenna
6. Rhine River
7. Rome

CHAPTER 7
LATE ANTIQUITY AND THE EMERGENCE OF THE MEDIEVAL WORLD

Chapter Outline

I. The Late Roman Empire
    A. Reforms of Diocletian and Constantine
        1. Political Reforms
        2. Military Reforms
        3. Economic and Social Trends
        4. Constantine's Building Program
    B. Empire's New Religion
        1. Conversion of Constantine
        2. Organization and Religious Disputes
            a. Bishops
            b. Heresies: Donatism and Arianism
    C. End of the Western Empire
        1. German Migrations
        2. German Threats
        3. Role of Masters of the Soldiers

II. The Germanic Kingdoms
    A. Ostrogothic Kingdom of Italy and Theodoric
    B. Visigothic Kingdom of Spain
    C. Frankish Kingdom
        1. Clovis and Catholicism
        2. Charles Martel
    D. Anglo-Saxon England
    E. Society of the Germanic Kingdoms
        1. Justice and *Wergeld*
        2. Frankish Families and Marriage

III. Development of the Christian Church
    A. Church Fathers
        1. Augustine and *The City of God*
        2. Jerome and the *Vulgate* Bible
    B. Power of the Pope
        1. Petrine Supremacy Theory
        2. Pope Leo I
    C. Church and State
        1. Example of Bishop Ambrose of Milan
        3. Pope Leo I and Attila the Hun

     D.   Gregory the Great

     E.   Monks and their Missions

       1. Saint Anthony

       2. Simeon the Stylite

       3. Communal Life

       4. Benedict and His Rule

       4. Women and the Rule

       5. Irish Monks as Missionaries

         a. Patrick in Ireland

         b. Columba in Iona

         c. Augustine and the Conversion of England

         d. Women and Monasticism

       6. Path of Celibacy

       7. Christian Intellectual Life in the Germanic Kingdoms

         a. Cassidorus: *Divine and Human Readings*

         b. Venerable Bede and *Ecclesiastical History of the English People*

IV. The Byzantine Empire

     A.   Reign of Justinian (527-565)

       1. Codification of Roman Law

       2. Intellectual Life under Justinian: Procopius' History

       3. Empress Theodora

       4. Justinian's Building Program: Hagia Sophia and Hippodrome

     B.   From Eastern Roman to Byzantine Empire

       1. Frontier Insecurity

       2. Byzantium in the Eighth Century

         a. Iconoclastic Controversy

         b. Emperor and Orthodoxy

         c. Separation from the West

V.   Rise of Islam

     A.   Muhammad

     B.   Teachings of Islam

       1. Quran

       2. Islam: Submission to Allah and *Hegira*

       3. "Five Pillars" and the *Shari'ah*

     C.   The Spread of Islam

       1. *Jihad*: Holy Wars of Conquest

       2. Shiites, Sunnites and Dynasties

       3. Victories over Byzantium

       4. Expansion Ends

Chapter Summary

With the decline of imperial Rome and its inability to maintain social and political order, reforms such a Diocletian and Constantine attempted to strength the aging structure. Diocletian divided the empire east from west, for better administration; and Constantine gave freedom of worship to Christians, in order to gain the support of that thriving population. Still the structure proved weak; and new peoples, orders, and religions stepped forward to fill the vacuum. In the West there were the Germanic kingdoms and the Roman Catholic Church. In the East there were the Byzantine Empire, the Orthodox Church, and Islam.

In what had been the Western Roman Empire, various Germanic tribes and the Catholic Church, once hostile to Rome, became its admirers and then its successors. The Germanic tribes which founded kingdoms in Italy, Spain, France, and Britain combined their own forms of government and society with those of the Roman world they conquered to form the medieval order. The Western Catholic Church built its success around an efficient organization which incorporated many Roman features and a militant claim that the Bishop of Rome, successor to Saint Peter, was the head of all Christian churches worldwide. The Catholic faith, once it had rid itself of early heresies, devised a strategy of missions, headed by monastic orders that eventually made all of Western Europe Christian. It held, in the imagery of Saint Augustine, that this world is a mere reflection of the invisible "City of God" that is eternal.

In what had been the Eastern Roman Empire, a new imperial order, headed by Justinian, emerged as the Byzantine Empire. In Byzantium, unlike the West, church and state were both under the emperor; and Byzantine society had a strength of unity but an absence of creative tension. Over the next thousand years Byzantium was whittled away until it was conquered by a new religion. Islam, founded by the Arab Muhammad, offered the people of the Near East and North Africa a message of submission to God as revealed through the life of a prophet and his teachings in the Qur'an. Islam occupied and reshaped many of the societies of the old Roman Empire. Christianity and Islam became rivals for the soul of Western man.

Learning Objectives

1. Be able to describe the reforms of Diocletian and Constantine and explain how they both extended the life of the empire and made its demise all the more likely.

2. Be able to describe both the role the Germanic tribes had in bringing down the Roman Empire and how they became its successors.

3. Be able to outline the major features of Germanic social and economic life, and show these features were used to erect a new socioeconomic system after the fall of Rome.

4. Be able to discuss the nature and scope of Byzantine culture and how it was able, against great odds, to perpetuate the Roman Empire in East for a thousand years after it fell in the West.

5. Be able to outline the major teachings of Muhammad, and show how they captured the imagination of a people who changed the Roman world.

Glossary of Names and Terms

1. Diocletian: Roman emperor who divided the empire East from West and changed its character forever.

2. Constantine: Roman emperor who reunited the empire for a brief time and gave legal status to the Christian faith.

3. Clovis: first king of the German Franks to be baptized a Christian, opening the way for his nation to be converted.

4. *Wergeld:* a fine levied by Germanic judges that required an offender to pay the family of someone he had wronged.

5. Vulgate: meaning common, this is the name for Jerome's translation of the Greek Bible into Latin, which became standard for the Western Catholic Church.

6. Benedict of Nursia: author of the *Rule* for monastic life which was adopted as standard for all Western Catholic monasteries, founder of the Benedictine Order.

7. Justianian: emperor of the Eastern Roman Empire, called Byzantium, who reclaimed lands lost to the Muslims and made Byzantium the envy of the world.

8. Hagia Sophia: Justinian's greatest religious edifice, a tribute to the Orthodox faith and the glory of his brief resurrection of Byzantine glory.

9. Allah: the word used by Muhammad to identify God, who he believed had chosen him as his last and greatest prophet and given him the final word of truth in Qur'an.

10. Jihad: a commonly misunderstood Arabic word, sometimes called a Holy War but in reality referring to the individual's struggle to find God.

Match the Following Words with their Definitions

1. Edict of Milan

2. Arius

3. Charles Martel

4. Augustine

5. Ambrose

6. Gregory I

7. Benedict of Nursia

8. Procopius

9. Hagia Sophia

10. Shi'ite

A. Historian of the Byzantine Empire

B. Prime example of Justinian's building program

C. Wrote *City of God*

D. Sent the first missionary to England

E. Gave legal recognition to the Christian religion

F.   Defeated Muslim army at Poitiers in 732

G.   Wrote the *Rule* for Western monasticism

H.   Questioned the divinity of Christ

I.   Follower of Muhammad's son-in-law Ali

J.   Established the pattern for bishops

Choose the Correct Answer

1.   Diocletian is remembered in history for having

   a.   Settled all border problems with barbarian tribes
   b.   Divided the empire into two parts, with himself as emperor of the East
   c.   Divided the empire into two parts, with himself keep the West
   d.   Given legal status to the small Christian community in Milan
   e.   Refused to retire at the end of his twenty year rule

2.   Constantine's Christian faith was

   a.   Deep and personal, since he took mass each day
   b.   Obviously just a ploy to win the support of the powerful Christian community
   c.   What made him execute people who would not join the Church
   d.   Consummated only when he was baptized near the end of his life
   e.   What held the Roman Empire together for another three centuries

3.   Theodoric's dream was to

   a.   Be crowned emperor by the Pope in the city of Rome
   b.   Marry a descendant of Julius Caesar
   c.   Codify the Roman Law
   d.   Forge a synthesis of Roman and Ostrogothic culture
   e.   Reunify the Roman Empire

4. Donatism's heresy lay in its insistence on the connection between

   a.   Priestly morality and the validity of sacraments
   b.   The Apostle Peter and the Roman papacy
   c.   Faith and reason
   d.   The two natures of Christ
   e.   Divine and human law

5.   What made Clovis different from previous Frankish rulers was the fact that he

   a.   Wrote odes to the Virgin Mary
   b.   Spoke and wrote fluent Latin
   c.   Was baptized a Roman Catholic Christian
   d.   Led his armies into battle
   e.   Enforced the principle of *wergeld*

73

6.   The Germanic *wergeld* was

    a.   Tax paid for goods imported from the Roman Empire
    b.   Compensatory payment for personal injury
    c.   A collection of fables and myths about the Nibelungen
    d.   A form of spiritual incantation
    e.   Money paid for a witness to support your testimony

7.   Frankish marriage customs

    a.   Prohibited sexual union for a year after marriage
    b.   Placed wives on equal legal footing with their husbands
    c.   Placed strong sanctions, even death, on adulterous women
    d.   Made divorce almost impossible to achieve
    e.   Put a higher fine on killing an old woman than on killing one of childbearing age

8.   Pope Gregory I encouraged

    a.   Missionary work among the Germanic tribes
    b.   Christian kings to give one-tenth of their lands to the Church
    c.   Parish priests to give up their wives
    d.   The Frankish king to annex the Papal States
    e.   The erection of a new Church of Saint Peter in Milan

9.   That form of monasticism that eventually was adopted in Western Europe stressed

    a.   Solitary living and masses only on Sunday
    b.   Pilgrimages to foreign holy shrines
    c.   Communal sharing of the Christian life
    d.   The Cult of the Virgin
    e.   Regard for the abbot over obedience to the Bishop of Rome

10.   When Celtic and Roman forms of Christianity collided in northern England

    a.   Roman Catholic structures and doctrine was victorious
    b.   The Celtic form triumphed
    c.   The two carved out separate but equal spheres of influence
    d.   There was bloody warfare across Britain
    e.   Many Britons returned to paganism

12.   Cassiodorus passed on to medieval scholarship the classical emphasis on

    a.   A Neoplatonic world of Ideas
    b.   A Christian Commonwealth of Nations
    c.   The Seven liberal arts
    d.   A Geocentric universe
    e.   The centrality of man in the universe

13. The Venerable Bede's *Ecclesiastical History*

    a.   Told the story of early Christian developments in Britain
    b.   Gave a clear rationale for Papal Supremacy over the Church
    d.   Detailed the circumstances of Ireland's conversion to Christianity
    d.   Argued that Christianity contributed to the fall of Rome
    e.   Condemned the heresies of Arianism and Donatism

14. Theodora played a crucial role in Justinian's reign when she helped him deal with

    a.   The Iconoclastic Controversy
    b.   A revolt of charioteers against his rule
    c.   His incompetent generals
    d.   The Arian heresy which threatened to divide the Orthodox church
    e.   His incipient impotence

15. Byzantine intellectual life strove to

    a.   Preserve and perpetuate the works of classical Greece
    b.   Produce literature that gave practical advice for living
    c.   Make breakthroughs in science
    d.   Provide people with entertainment and diversions
    e.   Explain the Christian mysteries to a cynical people

16. At the end of Justinian's reign Byzantium had

    a.   A stable, growing population
    b.   Frontiers secure against foreign invasion
    c.   Buildings that impressed the world
    d.   A full treasury that required few taxes on goods
    e.   No religious differences among its various groups

17. Eastern Emperor Leo III used the Iconoclastic Controversy to add

    a.   Lands in the west to his empire
    b.   Many Roman Catholic converts to the Orthodox Church
    c.   Precious icons to his own private collection
    d.   Prestige and power to his favored patriarch of Constantinople
    e.   New doctrines to the Code of Civil Theology

18. Muhammad believed Jews and Christians were

    a.   Infidels who should suffer for their perverse ways
    b.   Racially incapable of accepting Islam
    c.   Holders of part of the true faith
    d.   Eagerly awaiting his final revelation
    e.   Never going to accept Islam

19. The Qur'an is Islam's

    a.   Guide for living, revealed to Muhammad
    b.   Sacred shrine in Mecca, where the sacred stone is housed
    c.   Holy War against the infidel Christians and Jews
    d.   Tradition of making religious pilgrimages to holy shrine
    e.   Oral tradition, handed down from religious leaders through memorization

20. The Muslim leader Ali

    a.   Was Muhammad's son-in-law
    b.   Was assassinated by Muslim enemies
    c.   Inspired the Shi'ite Muslim movement
    d.   Is a controversial figure in Islam to the present day
    e.   All of the above

Complete the Following Sentences

1.   In Germanic law compurgation required that the accused swear an _____ and also be supported by _____ _____. The ordeal, on the other hand, depended upon _____ _____.

2.   The Council of _____ in 325 condemned _____ as a heresy and declared that Jesus was the _____ _____ as God.

3.   Gregory I established the papacy as a _____ _____ and began missionary work in _____ and _____.

4.   In his _____ for monastic life, which became standard in the West, Saint _____ was guided by the ideal of _____.

5.   The Irish monk _____ established a monastery off the coast of Scotland on the Isle of _____, from which he sent missionaries to covert the _____ and _____ of England.

6.   The Synod of Whitby settled the differences between _____ and _____ Christianity, leading in time to a gradual _____ of the two.

7.   In his great work ___ _____ __ _____, Augustine created a Christian philosophy of _____ and _____.

8.   Justinian's great contributions to Western civilization were his _____ _____ and the building of _____ _____

9.   Iconoclasts sought to abolish _____ _____ because they considered them _____.

10.   Muhammad's flight in 622 from _____ to _____ established the Muslim practice of _____.

Place the Following in Chronological Order and Give Dates

1.	Clovis is converted to Christianity	1.
2.	Bede completes his *Ecclesiastical History*	2.
3.	Hagia Sophia is completed	3.
4.	Charles Martel defeats the Muslims	4.
5.	Visigoths sack Rome	5.
6.	Justinian codifies the Roman law	6.
7.	Odoacer deposes Romulus Augustulus	7.

Questions for Critical Thought

1. Examine the reforms of Diocletian and Constantine, and show how they did and did not solve the problems of the Roman Empire. How did they change it forever?

2. Define heresy, and give examples of it in the early Christian church. Why were heresies considered such a threat to the Church's well being?

3. Explain how the Germanic tribes and their energetic way of life combined with Roman culture to create the medieval world. Describe that new world.

4. How did the Bishop of Rome become in fact as well as in theory the central figure in the Roman Catholic Church? What role did Leo I and Gregory I play in it?

5. Discuss the monastic movement that swept the church in the first few centuries after Christ. What did its life offer young people in a world that seemed to be falling apart? What long term effects did it have on the Church?

6. Outline the part played by monks in the conversion of Europe to Christianity. Give examples using the more prominent ones, and show what they accomplished.

7. How did the Eastern Empire (Byzantium) differ from the tribal societies that replaced the Western Empire at the other end of the Mediterranean? Which was truer to the Roman model?

8. Describe the religion and culture of Islam. Discuss its origins, its conquest of a large part of the civilized world, and its immediate and permanent impact on Western Civilization.

Analysis of Primary Source Documents

1. Compare the two descriptions you have read of the Huns. Why are there such differences between the two accounts? Why does the Ammianus account contain such exaggerations?

2. Define the word "civilitas" as people of the late ancient world understood it. Why did men like Theodoric hold it in such high regard?

3. Describe the Germanic "ordeal" and speculate on the logic of it. What kind of society would choose it as a way to achieve justice? Is it, in modified form, still a part of our modern legal system?

4. Recount the conversion of Saint Augustine. What clues do you get as to why he later became such an influential figure in the early Christian church?

5. If the spiritual biographies of early Christian monks were meant to inspire model behavior in the average Christian, what personal characteristics would the life of Saint Anthony have taught readers to imitate?

6. After reading Cummean, what conclusions can you draw about early Irish Christianity's attitude human sexuality? Would most modern people consider it healthy? Explain.

7. Show how Bede, in his life of Abbess Hilda, sought to teach moral "lessons" and yet took care to be historically accurate.

8. After reading the selection from the Qur'an, try to account for its appeal, in the Middle Ages and down to the present, to followers of Muhammad.

CHAPTER 8
EUROPEAN CIVILIZATION
IN THE EARLY MIDDLE AGES,
750-1000

Chapter Outline

I. Europeans and the Environment
    A. Farming
    B. Climate

II. World of the Carolingians
    A. Charlemagne and the Carolingian Empire (768-814)
        1. Charlemagne's Expansionism
            a. Into Spain
            b. Into Germany
        2. Governing the Empire
            a. Messengers of the King
            b. Uses of the Church
        3. Charlemagne as Emperor
            a. Coronation
            b. Significance
    C. Carolingian Intellectual Renewal
        1. Scriptoria
        2. Carolingian Minuscule
        3. Alcuin
    D. Life in the Carolingian World
        1. Family and Marriage
        2. Christianity and Sexuality
        3. New Attitudes toward Children
        4. Travel and Hospitality
        5. Diet
            a. Water and Wine
            b. Physicians

III. Disintegration of the Carolingian Empire
    A. Invasions of the Ninth and Tenth Centuries
        1. Muslims and Magyars from the East
        2. Vikings from the North

IV. The Emerging World of Lords and Vassals
   A. Vassalage
   B. Fief-Holding
      1. Mutual Obligations
   C. New Political Configurations in the Tenth Century
      1. Eastern Franks: Otto I and a New "Roman Empire"
      2. Western Franks: Hugh Capet and France
      3. Alfred the Great and Anglo-Saxon England
   E. Manorial System

V. The Zenith of Byzantine Civilization
   A. Macedonian Dynasty

VI. Slavic Peoples of Central and Eastern Europe
   A. Western Slavs
   B. Southern Slavs
   C. Eastern Slavs

VII. The Expansion of Islam
   A. Abbasid Dynasty
   B. Islamic Civilization
      1. Bagdad's "House of Wisdom"
      2. Avicenna

Chapter Summary

Medieval Europe emerged from the rubble of the Western Roman Empire in the late eighth century. Its founders were the Carolingian monarchs of the Germanic tribe that had settled in Gaul, the Franks, and at its center was the figure of Charlemagne.

The first of the Carolingian kings of the Franks, Pepin the Short, son of the warrior Charles Martel, gained his throne by making a mutually-beneficial alliance with the Bishop of Rome. On Christmas Day, 800, Pepin's son and heir, Charlemagne, was crowned emperor by Pope Leo III in Rome. Then and there the Middle Ages began to take shape.

Charlemagne's empire was Catholic, expansionist, and as enlightened as circumstances allowed. While Charlemagne forcibly converted the tribes he conquered to Christianity, he also built churches, schools, and governmental agencies to give his subjects a better way of life. It was not until a generation after Charlemagne's death that the world he had created began to decline—and then only temporarily. His three grandsons divided his empire; and foreign raiders did their marauding worst; but after a period of struggle, the Carolingian system reasserted itself. The medieval world that emerged was feudal and manorial, it was Christian, and it vested power in the hands of lords who were expected to keep order.

In the meantime, the Eastern Roman Empire, Byzantium, experienced one last moment of glory and grandeur before beginning a decline toward eventual dissolution. At the same time the Slavic peoples of Eastern Europe began consolidating under Viking lords to form a Russian state, which imitated Byzantium. Islam, though divided into nation-states that sometimes warred among themselves, began creating urban societies known for their high education and culture. Across Europe, east to west, change was in the air.

Learning Objectives

1.   Be able to trace the formation of the Carolingian Empire and explain the significance of Charlemagne's coronation by the Pope in 800.

2.   Be able to discuss the characteristics and achievements of the Carolingian intellectual renewal and its effect on the European Middle Ages.

3.   Be able to explain the reasons vassalage and the manorial system developed, how they addressed medieval circumstances, and their long lasting effects on European society.

4.   Be able to describe the Byzantine Empire's development between 750 and 1000, and show how it influenced the rising peoples of Central and Eastern Europe.

5.   Be able to trace the development of Islamic civilization between 750 and 1000, particularly accounting for its influence in the intellectual world.

Glossary of Names and Terms

1.   Pepin: first Carolingian king of the Franks, anointed by a representative of the Pope, creating a lasting alliance with the Catholic Church.

2.   *Missi Dominici*: literally "messengers of the king," sent out from Charlemagne's court to ensure that local lords were administering their lands in accord with the wishes of the king.

3.   Leo III: Pope who on Christmas Day, 800, crowned Charlemagne Emperor of the Romans.

4.   Alcuin: director of Charlemagne's palace school, he required the use of classical Latin and a seven part liberal arts curriculum.

5.   Otto I: the most successful of the Saxon dynasty that ruled the eastern Franks after the Carolingian demise, he depended on clerical assistants rather than lay lords to administer his realm.

6.   Hugh Capet: member of the House of Capet, lord of the lands around modern day Paris, he was chosen king of the western Franks and established a lasting dynasty.

7.   Alfred the Great: King of Wessex who defeated the Danes and prepared the way for a united English kingdom, encouraging the translation of classical works into the vernacular.

8.   Photius: Patriarch of the Eastern Orthodox Church who condemned the Bishop of Rome as a heretic and further widened the schism between the Eastern and Western churches.

9.   Vladimir: leader of the Rus who married a Byzantine emperor's sister and adopted Orthodox Christianity as the official religion of Kiev.

10.   Avicenna: Muslim scholar Ibn Sina who wrote the encyclopedia that became standard for medieval medical students.

Match the Following Words with their Definitions

1. *Missi Dominici*

2. Carolingian minuscule

3. Charles the Bald

4. Lothair

5. Homage

6. Fief

7. Ile-de-France

8. Alfred the Great

9. Photius

10. Avicenna

A. Private holdings of the Capets

B. Eastern Patriarch who excommunicated the pope

C. Charlemagne's administrators

D. King of Wessex who made peace with the Danes

E. Author of a medieval medical encyclopedia

F. Inheritor of Charlemagne's western lands

G. Form of writing for the first post-Roman intellectual revival

H. Grandson of Charlemagne who inherited the title emperor

I. A lord's benefice to his vassal

J. Willing recognition of dependency

Choose the Correct Answer

1.   Charlemagne's key to holding power was his

     a.   Reform of the Catholic Church
     b.   Efficient system of taxation
     c.   Widespread administrative bureaucracy
     d.   Ability to inspire his people's loyalty
     e.   Ability to control his sons

2.   The expansion of the Carolingian Empire under Charlemagne

     a.   Was carried out by the largest army in all of history
     b.   Was most successful against the Germanic tribes to the east
     c.   Resulted in the quick and easy defeat of the Saxons
     d.   Resulted in the annexation of all Europe except Italy
     e.   Had its easiest victories in Spain

3.   Charlemagne converted the eastern Germanic tribes to Christianity by means of

     a.   Luxurious gifts, including women, to local kings
     b.   His skill in theological debate
     c.   Brutal military force
     d.   Monastic missionaries loyal to the king
     e.   Preachers who frightened the Saxons of hell fire

4.   On Christmas Day, 800, Pope Leo III crowned Charlemagne emperor because

     a.   Of a vision from God
     b.   The constitution of Classical Rome demanded it
     c.   The lord-vassal relationship encouraged it
     d.   Charlemagne had protected him from his enemies
     e.   He thought it would lead to a war against Islam

5.   The "Carolingian Renaissance" refers primarily to the revival of

     a.   Classical studies of the seven liberal arts
     b.   Christian missionary ventures into pagan lands
     c.   Roman military tactics in battles against the Saxons
     d.   Trade and commerce across Europe
     e.   The celebration of the human body in art

6.   Scholarship in the Carolingian Empire was characterized by

     a.   Literary creativity using original thought
     b.   Illuminated manuscripts done in Merovingian cursive
     c.   A rejection of all classical references to pagan gods
     d.   Reproductions of manuscripts in Benedictine *scriptoria*
     e.   An emphasis on writing in the vernacular Gothic languages

Chapter 8

7. The Church's impact upon Frankish marriage and family customs led to the

   a. Wife's control of the nuclear household
   b. Dominance of the extended family
   c. Acceptance of common law marriages
   d. Extinction of all infanticide
   e. End of all adulterous affairs

8. Regarding sexuality, the Roman Catholic Church of the Early Middle Ages

   a. Failed to enforce complete clerical celibacy
   b. Continued to call for the death penalty for homosexuality
   c. Said sex for pleasure was permissible only in marriage
   d. Accepted coitus interruptus as the only legitimate form of birth control
   e. Forbade women to admit they experience pleasure in sexual intercourse

9. In the early Middle Ages, the Church treated homosexuality

   a. As a crime punishable by death
   b. As a violation of the natural law
   c. Less harshly than the use of contraceptives by married couples
   d. Less harshly than having sex with animals
   e. More harshly than the laws of Justinian required

10. The early medieval Church encouraged people to

    a. Use herbal medicines to prevent conception
    b. Leave unwanted children at monasteries and convents
    c. Pressure their rulers to build public orphanages
    d. Have sexual relations only on prescribed days
    e. Abort fetuses if the mother's life were threatened

11. Which of the following statements best applies to the Carolingian diet?

    a. Beef and mutton made up the largest part of the upper class diet
    b. Bread, vegetables, and spices dominated the diets of all classes
    c. Ale was the favored beverage of all classes
    d. A deficiency in calories and carbohydrates caused many people to fall prey to diseases
    e. Sugar began to be commonly used after trade routes opened with the East

12. The significance of the Treaty of Verdun was that it

    a. Created the permanent divisions of Europe
    b. Led to civil unrest among divided populations
    c. Was the first treaty successfully overruled by a pope
    d. Violated the explicit instructions of Charlemagne's will
    e. Made the Saxons subject to Charles the Bald

13. The Vikings began to be civilized when

    a. Scandinavian kings established universities
    b. The Latin language became dominant in their lands
    c. They accepted the Christian faith
    d. The Franks gave them land grants along the coast of the English Channel
    e. Medical advances cured them of their chronic wanderlust

14. The lord-vassal relationship of medieval Europe

    a. Marked a distinct departure from the traditional German economic system
    b. Forbade hereditary fiefdoms
    c. Was a benign form of economic slavery
    d. Was an honorable relationship between free men
    e. Brought an end to the Roman world of free trade

15. In the economic structure of the Early Middle Ages

    a. Feudalism replaced manorialism
    b. Almost the entire free peasant class become serfs
    c. The economy was predominantly agrarian
    d. Tribes gave way to centralized society
    e. Women were much more powerful than they had been in Roman days

16. French nobles expected their king Hugh Capet to

    a. Defend them against all invaders
    b. Live off the revenues of his private lands
    c. Enforce Christian law and morality
    d. Provide great banquets and tournaments for their pleasure
    e. Create a strong central government

17. Photius excommunicated the Bishop of Rome for

    a. Departing from the doctrine of the Nicene Creed
    b. Encouraging the King of France to invade Italy
    c. Calling for a crusade against Islam
    d. His immoral personal life
    e. Challenging the Patriarch's claim to be head of the Catholic Church

18. The "Rus," who gave their name to Russia, were

    a. Intellectuals educated in Constantinople
    b. A red haired tribe of Slavs
    c. Rough uncivilized people from Scandinavia
    d. Direct lineal descendants of Charlemagne
    e. Cattle thieves, from which we get the term "rustlers"

19. The "House of Wisdom" in Baghdad preserved
    a. The earliest known map of the world
    b. Muhammad's skull
    c. The true family tree of Muhammad Ali
    d. Works of Plato and Aristotle
    e. Chinese medical encyclopedias

20. The Muslim scholar Ibn Sina showed that

    a. Algebra opens doors to more attractive architectural forms
    b. The earth is round
    c. Disease can be spread by contaminated water
    d. Free markets make for greater prosperity
    e. Islam is the most advanced of religions

Complete the Following Sentences

1. Charlemagne's biographer _____ described the Saxons as a _____ people who worshipped _____.

2. A new European civilization was symbolically born on Christmas Day, 800, with coronation of _____ by Pope _____ in the city of _____.

3. Carolingian scholars pioneered in the field of writing by their invention of the _____, a form of _____ much easier to read than the old _____ cursive.

4. The Treaty of Verdun in 843 divided Charlemagne's empire between his three grandsons: _____, _____, and _____.

5. The Muslim raids on Christendom during the ninth century were most successful on the island of _____; the Magyars took over the plains of _____; while Vikings won for themselves a duchy in France called _____.

6. The Anglo-Saxon king who defeated the Danish invaders was _____, king of _____ in _____ England.

7. When the Bishop of Rome accepted a revision of the _____ Creed, the Eastern Patriarch _____ excommunicated him for heresy, thus creating a _____ in the Christian Church.

8. The Viking Rurik, leader of a band called the _____, established a capital at _____ in 862, and his successor Oleg created the Principality of _____.

9. After his conversion to Christianity, the Russian prince _____ sought to have his country imitate the _____ and _____ ideals of the _____ Empire.

10. Muslim scholars were respected in the West for their original and valuable contributions to the fields of _____, _____, and _____.

Place the Following in Chronological Order and Give Dates

1.	Treaty of Verdun	1.	
2.	Alfred makes peace with the Danes	2.	
3.	Vladimir's conversion to Christianity	3.	
4.	Charlemagne crowned emperor	4.	
5.	Reign of Pepin over the Franks	5.	
6.	Michael III begins to reign in Byzantium	6.	
7.	Charlemagne's conquest of the Saxons	7.	

Questions for Critical Thought

1. Give details of how Charlemagne expanded the frontiers of his Frankish lands. How did the expansion change his empire?

2. Discuss the long-range significance of Charlemagne's coronation by the pope and the belief that he was a new Roman emperor, or "King of Europe."

3. Explain why marriage became a central concern of the Catholic Church. How did its policies influence the institution of marriage throughout the Middle Ages?

4. What surprised you about the diet and hygiene of the various classes in the Carolingian era? With your modern knowledge, what advice would you give them?

5. Discuss the system known as feudalism. Show how it responded to and attempted to solve the social problems of its day. In what ways did it succeed and in what ways did it fail?

6. Compare and contrast the importance of Otto I and Hugh Capet for the two nations that each helped establish.

7. Discuss the relationship of the Slavic peoples of Eastern Europe to the Germanic peoples of Western Europe in their formative days. How do those relationships continue today, and what are the consequences?

8. Explain how Islamic culture continued to develop after the death of Muhammad. What contributions, positive and negative, did it make to Western Europe?

Chapter 8

Analysis of Primary Source Documents

1. Show how Einhard organized his material to portray Charlemagne as the ideal leader. What probable exaggerations do you detect?

2. Describe the way a young man called to serve an early medieval king was supposed to conduct himself. Why at this time might a mother be the one to teach her son these lessons?

3. Summarize the medicinal prescriptions commonly given in Anglo-Saxon England. Choose three examples that show them to be, for their day, progressive and scientific; and choose three that show them to be neither.

4. How do you know, from the terms they use, that the writers of the Anglo-Saxon Chronicle were churchmen? How do they interpret the actions of the Vikings in their land?

5. Describe the relationship—the benefits and the responsibilities—between a medieval lord and his vassal. Explain why and how this relationship, with its obligations, was the key to the feudal system.

6. Discuss some of the concerns of suppliants before medieval manorial law courts. Does the justice rendered seem fair by today's standards?

7. Recount the visit of Liudprand of Cremona to the Byzantine court of Constantine VII. Explain why future historians, reading such accounts, would give the adjective "Byzantine" its modern connotation.

8. Summarize Ibn Fadlan's impressions of the Rus he met. What did he find offensive, and what do such things tell us about the Muslim society from which he came?

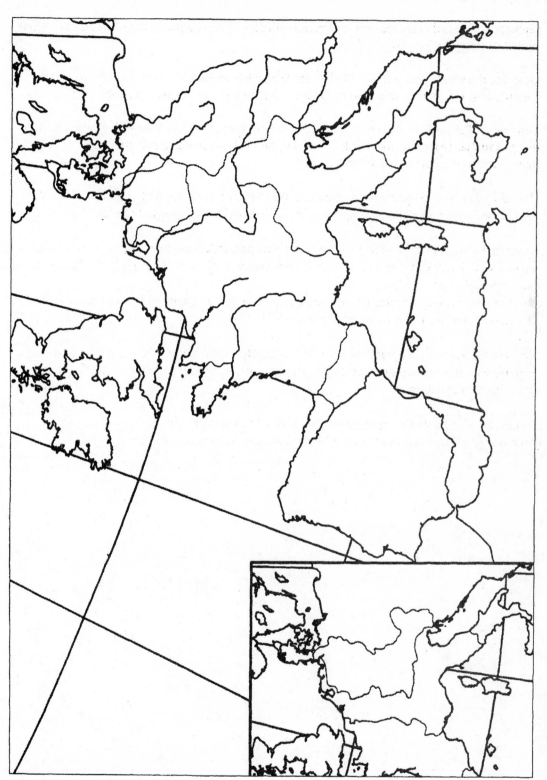

Map Exercise 5

Map Exercise 5: The Carolingian Empire

Shade and label the following

1. Aquitaine
2. Baltic Sea
3. Bavaria
4. Burgundy
5. North Sea
6. Papal States
7. Saxony
8. Spanish March
9. Umayyd Kingdom of Spain
10. Wessex

Pinpoint and label the following

1. Aachen
2. Barcelona
3. Milan
4. Paris
5. Rome
6. Toledo

(Inset) Shade the following

1. Kingdom of Charles the Bald
2. Kingdom of Lothair
3. Kingdom of Louis the German

CHAPTER 9
THE RECOVERY AND GROWTH OF EUROPEAN SOCIETY IN THE HIGH MIDDLE AGES

Chapter Outline

I.   Land and People in the High Middle Ages
    A.   New Agriculture
        1.   Improvement in the Climate
        2.   Expansion of Arable Lands
        3.   New Plow: *Carruca*
        4.   Watermill
        5.   Three-Field System
        6.   Free-Peasant Labor
    B.   Life of the Peasantry
        1.   Seasons
        2.   Holidays and the Village Church
        3.   Household, Family, and the Role of Women
        4.   Diet
    C.   Aristocracy of the High Middle Ages
        1.   Men of War and Church Attempts to Curb Violence
        2.   Castles
        3.   Aristocratic Women: Eleanor of Aquitaine, Blanche of Castile
        4.   Knighthood: Way of the Warrior
        6.   Role of Tournaments
    D.   Marriage Patterns of the Aristocracy

II. New World of Trade and Cities
    A.   Revival of Trade
        1.   Italy
        2.   Flanders
    B.   Growth of Cities
        1.   New Cities and Citizens: Burghers
        2.   Charters of Rights
        3.   City Governments
    C.   Life in the Medieval City
        1.   Pollution and Crime
        2.   Apprenticeship
    D.   Industry in Medieval Cities

III. Intellectual and Artistic World of the High Middle Ages
    A.   Rise of Universities
        1.   Cathedral Schools
        2.   Bologna's School of Law
        3.   University of Paris
        4.   Oxford and Cambridge

B. Teaching in the Medieval University
    1. Lectures
    2. *Artium Baccularius*, *Artium Magister*
C. Students in the Medieval University: Learning and Violence
D. Revival of Classical Antiquity
    1. Greek Science and Philosophy
    2. Islamic Influences: Averroes
E. Development of Scholasticism
    1. Peter Abelard
    2. Universals
    3. Thomas Aquinas
F. Revival of Roman Law
G. Literature in the High Middle Ages
    1. Latin Poetry
    2. Vernacular Literature: Troubadours
H. Romanesque Architecture: "A White Marble of Churches"
    1. Basilica Form
    2. Barrel Vaults and Heavy Walls
I. Gothic Cathedrals
    1. Ribbed Vaults and Pointed Arches
    2. Flying Buttresses and Stained Glass
    3. Community Construction

Chapter Summary

Medieval European society was primarily a rural civilization, with most people living as serfs on the lands of lords. Yet new agricultural techniques permitted the population to grow steadily, despite a high infant mortality rate; and the manorial system kept a relatively high degree of social stability and order. The life of the peasant revolved around his family, his village, and his church.

It was a society ruled by aristocrats, the great, powerful families of Europe. Noble families ruled both cities and rural areas, training their daughters for the responsibilities of advantageous marriages and their sons to fight in defense of church and king. At the top of the aristocratic pyramid, a handful of families ruled kingdoms that grew ever more united and prosperous.

A dramatic revival in trade led to the growth of medieval cities. Rising on the sites of Roman towns and trade fairs, often near easily defended hill-top castles, they continually expanded their protective walls as they grew. They increased overall prosperity, gave impetus to the arts, and trained their residents in specialized skills that led to even more prosperity.

There was also an intellectual and cultural "warming" across the Western world. Universities were founded and given royal sanctions in Italy, France, England, and Spain, training young men for careers in theology, law, and medicine. The Scholastic philosophers who lectured and debated at the universities, such men as Peter Abelard and Thomas Aquinas, gave to the High Middle Ages an intellectual dignity seldom matched in any age. Literature took on a renewed energy, both in classical Latin and in the vernacular of the nation-states. Architecture moved from Romanesque to Gothic, creating a sense of grandeur that clearly demonstrated the triumph of the medieval Church. This was no "dark age."

Learning Objectives

1. Be able to describe the way of life and practical functions of the aristocracy in the High Middle Ages.

2. Be able to discuss the impact of the revival of trade in the High Middle Ages, how it changed Europe and prepared for the modern age.

3. Be able to trace the development of the medieval city, how it coped with its problems, what it gave to the overall society, including Scholastic Philosophy.

4. Be able to describe why and how the medieval universities began and the impact they had on the various nations where they thrived.

5. Be able to give the major themes of literature and the styles of architecture of the High Middle Ages and why this age is celebrated for their achievements.

Glossary of Names and Terms

1. *Aratum*: the plow used by farmers in Southern Europe, which proved inadequate for work in the North, replaced there by the *carruca*.

2. Peace of God: instituted and encouraged by the Church as a way of curtailing medieval warriors from attacking churches, clergy, and civilians, limiting the fighting to knights.

3. Chivalry: the way of life for aristocratic warriors, men on horseback, which gradually became a way of civilized behavior toward women and religious institutions.

4. *Commune*: a medieval association of town dwellers to assure their rights against the power of lay or ecclesiastical lords.

5. Journeyman: a medieval craftsman, on a level between an apprentice and a master, who was paid wages for assisting a master until he could himself become one.

6. *Artium magister*: the second degree, after *artium baccalaureus*, a medieval student sought to earn, giving the person a license to teach.

7. Scholasticism: the theological and philosophical system and method of medieval universities, now considered among the high points of logical thought.

8. Thomas Aquinas: Scholastic philosopher whose systematic work came closest to a reconciliation of faith and reason, later the basis for modern Catholic theology.

9. Troubadour: a poet whose works dealt with themes of courtly love, in which an unattainable lady inspires a young knight to deeds of courage.

10. Gothic: architectural term used to describe the most successful of high medieval church styles, with high ceilings, thin walls, and stained glass windows to let in the divine light.

Chapter 9

Match the Following Words with their Definitions

1. *Carruca*

2. Pentecost

3. Eleanor of Aquitaine

4. Chivalry

5. Flanders

6. *Burgus*

7. Margery Kempe

8. Trivium

9. *Summa Theologica*

10. Troubadour

A. Ideals of the aristocratic warrior

B. Famous brewer

C. Region where medieval trade first revived

D. Holy Day for celebrating the gift of the Holy Spirit

E. Masterpiece of Scholasticism

F. Basic level of university study

G. Medieval agricultural instrument

H. Poetry of courtly love

I. Medieval walled city

J. Consort of two kings

Choose the Correct Answer

1. The dramatic increase in the European population between 1000 and 1300

    a. Occurred despite negative climatic conditions
    b. Especially benefited women of child-bearing age
    c. Can in part be attributed to greater agricultural yields
    d. Led to populations with many more women than men
    e. Caused wars over limited food supplies

2. A negative result of the new agricultural methods of the Middle Ages was

    a. The disappearance of many forests
    b. Pollution of most small streams
    c. Periodic severe famines
    d. Attacks on isolated farmers by wild animals
    e. Pesticide poisoning in urban populations

3. A social innovation associated with the new medieval agriculture was

    a. The town and market agricultural council
    b. A significantly freer peasantry
    c. Domesday Codes in each country
    d. Hourly wages for labor
    e. Crowding into cities due to joblessness in the countryside

4. The medieval village church

    a. Strongly condemned lingering pagan practices
    b. Competed with pagan religions for converts
    c. Celebrated over fifty holy days each year
    d. Forbade economic pursuits on holy ground
    e. Had celibate priests

5. The medieval peasant ate

    a. A wide variety of vegetables
    b. Better than most Romans during the decline of the empire
    c. Mutton or cheese every Sunday
    d. Fresh meat only on feast days
    e. Fish every Friday

6. Aristocrats of the High Middle Ages

    a. Were divided into two classes: knights and nobles
    b. Were prohibited from fighting among themselves
    c. Had all their warring energies diverted by the Church into charitable work
    d. Were regarded as "defenders of society"
    e. Always defended the innocent against aggressors

7. The nobles of the High Middle Ages

    a. Were preoccupied with warfare
    b. Were preoccupied with business endeavors
    c. Shunned warfare altogether
    d. Spent their time managing their estates
    e. Traveled to foreign countries in search of relics

8. The growing independence of medieval urban areas was due in large part to

    a. Victories of their armies over lords and bishops
    b. Encouragement from bishops and abbots
    c. The huge populations they had to protect
    d. Revival of trade and commerce and their growing wealth
    e. A rise in urban diseases that made lords afraid to enter them

9. Which of the following statements best describes medieval international trade?

    a. The Church's prohibition against profit retarded mercantile growth
    b. The "putting out" system of commercial capitalism had no effect on the woolen industry
    c. The growth of mercantile activity led to the growth of Italian banking
    d. The commercial revolution was largely caused by the pioneering genius of merchants in Germany
    e. European merchants traded more with Muslims than with fellow Christians

10. Cities in medieval Europe

    a. Were ruled by lords under a manorial system
    b. Rivaled those of the Arabs and Byzantium
    c. Attained privileges through the work of communes
    d. Depended little on the surrounding countryside for supplies
    e. Harbored heretics and criminals

11. Communes in France and England differed from those in Italy by

    a. Having open, democratic elections of officials
    b. Being subject to royal authority
    c. Being under the absolute rule of a mayor
    d. Having the right to exercise capital punishment
    e. Being limited by royal decree from growing past a certain population

12. Craft apprentices

    a. Received only room and board from their masters for their work
    b. Were always blood relatives of the masters for whom they worked
    c. Joined trade unions during their second year of apprenticeship
    d. Received regular wages and benefits
    e. Moved directly to masters in their third year

13. Throughout Europe in the Twelfth Century

    a. A tremendous intellectual optimism and energy took charge
    b. Scholars replaced Latin with Greek as the language of universities
    c. Scholars felt they had reconciled classical philosophy with Christian theology
    d. There was talk of a western passage to the New World
    e. Scandals erupted over pedophilia in ecclesiastical schools

14. The universities of the High Middle Ages

    a. Were modeled on the schools of Greece and Rome
    b. Represented a distinct departure from earlier cathedral schools
    c. Began with an experimental college at Cambridge
    d. Were agents of peace within boisterous medieval cities
    e. First admitted only boys but gradually opened doors to girls

15. Students in medieval universities

    a. Came strictly from the aristocratic classes
    b. Began their education at age 25, after serving several years as priests
    c. Often engaged in violent confrontations with townspeople
    d. Were both male and female
    e. Lived like monks, eschewing alcohol and sex

16. The life of Peter Abelard was dedicated to

    a. Strict observance of poverty, chastity, and obedience
    b. Disproving church dogma without being charged with heresy
    c. The modern application of Roman law
    d. Using dialectical reasoning to reconcile the Scripture with the Church Fathers
    e. Deflowering the maidens he was hired to tutor

17. Which of the following statements best characterizes Thomas Aquinas?

    a. He taught that human reason is too weak to be trusted
    b. He considered human reason to be the link between the natural and the spiritual worlds
    c. He said that everything in God's creation is perfect
    d. He depended purely on human reason, disparaging divine revelation
    e. He depended heavily on the writings of Plato to illuminate Christian theology

18. By the middle of the twelfth century "doctors of law" were

    a. Writing systematic commentaries
    b. Defending new medical practices in courts
    c. Serving in the courts of kings
    d. Expelled from most universities
    e. Medical advisers to judges

19. One favorite theme of twelfth century poetry throughout Europe was the

    a.   Love affair of Abelard and Heloise
    b.   Tragedy of King Arthur of Britain
    c.   Military career of Frederick I of the Holy Roman Empire
    d.   Love affair of Antony and Cleopatra
    e.   Journey of an Acadian youth searching for his Evangeline

19. Gothic cathedrals were built

    a.   Without windows to create dark, quiet places to meditate
    b.   For the glory of kings and their consorts
    c.   By entire communities contributing their labor
    d.   By master masons who practiced secret rituals
    e.   Usually within the lifetimes of the architects who designed them

Complete the Following Sentences

1. Medieval agricultural practices changed for the better when farmers abandoned the _____, a light Mediterranean plow, for the _____, which helped soil to _____.

2. The three most important feast days of the medieval Church were _____, _____, and _____; but other holy days were dedicated to various _____, particularly to the _____ _____.

3. A medieval castle was both a residential palace for a _____ _____ and a _____ _____ in time of trouble.

4. Eleanor of Aquitaine was married first to _____ of France, with whom she went on a _____ to Palestine, and later to _____ of England, whose _____ she helped revolt against him.

5. Medieval townspeople who had trouble gaining _____ of liberty from local lords at times formed _____ in order to bargain collectively.

6. Margery Kempe, daughter of a _____, made and sold her own _____, thus proving that a medieval woman could gain a degree of economic _____.

7. A person aspiring to learn a trade in late medieval society served first as an _____ to a _____ _____, then was a _____ until he had produced his first _____.

8. The first three medieval universities were at _____ in Italy, _____ in France, and _____ in England, where the most common method of instruction was the _____.

9. Peter Abelard, the great _____ philosopher, was punished for his love affair with _____ by being _____.

10. Thomas Aquinas' great work, _____ _____, addressed _____ controversial issues, using the _____ _____.

Place the Following in Chronological Order and Give Dates

1. Frederick I founds university at Bologna   1.

2. Oxford founded   2.

3. Eleanor's sons revolt against their father   3.

4. Death of Thomas Aquinas   4.

5. Revolt in Laon   5.

6. Suger finds the tall beams   6.

7. Death of Peter Abelard   7.

Questions for Critical Thought

1. Explain how a typical medieval city was governed. Where did real political power lie, and who benefited from it?

2. What kind and level of public hygiene did the typical medieval city have? What essential services were lacking, and how did councils go about supplying them?

3. What did the medieval guilds do for the cities? What would have been lacking in the cities without them?

4. Describe the way medieval universities were founded, the curricula they followed, and the kind of life students pursued in university towns. In what ways was medieval university life worse, and better, than university life today?

5. What concerned the scholastic philosophers of the Late Middle Ages? How did some of the major figures resolve the questions raised by these concerns?

6. What caused the "renaissance of the twelfth century," what did it accomplish, and what were its legacies? How does it compare with other high points in Western history?

7. What were the major interests of the literary figures of the High Middle Ages? What forms and styles did the writers adopt and adapt to express their thoughts?

8. What does the Gothic cathedral tell you about the skills and values of medieval man? Why do we still admire their work so much?

Chapter 9

Analysis of Primary Source Documents

1. What does the story of Abbot Suger and his timbers tell you about the treatment of forests and other natural resources the High Middle Ages?

2. What seems to have been the consensus among medieval men, as demonstrated by the two men's writings you have read, about medieval women? What does this say about the women of the day—and the men?

3. Compare the attitude toward trade of the biographer of Godric with that of the Muslim Ibn Khaldun. Why during this early period of commercial revival would one writer see it as a means to good and the other an inherently dishonest enterprise?

4. What happened in the communal revolt in Laon? What caused it, and what were its results? What does it tell you about life in medieval cities?

5. Compare and contrast medieval city problems, including pollution, with those of our own cities. How much more or less likely are we to solve our problems today than the King of England was to solve those of Boutham? Explain.

6. Speculate on the conditions of life in the medieval university towns that would lead to the kind of riot Oxford experienced. Show how each side was right and each wrong.

7. What percentage of Thomas Aquinas' opinion about the formation of woman is logic, what part Church doctrine, and what part contemporary prejudice?

8. Roland was a hero and role model for medieval aristocrats. From the song about his life, show the masculine qualities medieval men admired. How do they resemble and how are they different from the qualities men admire today?

Map Exercise 6

Map Exercise 6: Cultural Centers in Medieval Europe

Shade and label the following

1. Baltic Sea
2. Denmark
3. England
4. France
5. Holy Roman Empire
6. Ireland
7. Italy
8. North Sea
9. Scotland
10. Spain

Pinpoint and label the following

1. Avignon
2. Bologna
3. Cambridge
4. Canterbury
5. Chartres
6. Cluny
7. Florence
8. London
9. Monte Cassino
10. Oxford
11. Paris
12. Rome
13. Salamanca
14. Vienna

CHAPTER 10
THE RISE OF KINGDOMS AND THE GROWTH OF CHURCH POWER

Chapter Outline

I. Emergence and Growth of European Kingdoms, 1000-1300
   A. England in the High Middle Ages
      1. William the Conqueror and Norman England
      2. Ties with France
      3. The Plantagenet Henry II
         a. Financial Reform
         b. Conflicts with the Church and Thomas Becket
      4. King John and *Magna Carta*
      5. Edward I and the Birth of Parliament
   B. Growth of the French Kingdom
      1. Capetians
      2. Philip II Augustus
      3. Saint Louis IX and Justice
      4. Philip IV (the Fair) and the Estates-General
   C. Christian Reconquest: The Spanish Kingdoms
   D. Lands of the Holy Roman Empire: Germany and Italy
      1. Imperial Weakness and the Exploitation of Italy
      2. Normans
      3. Frederick I Barbarossa
      4. Frederick II
   E. New Kingdoms in Northern and Eastern Europe
      1. Scandinavia
      2. Hungary and Poland
      3. Mongol Empire
      4. Kiev and Russia
         a. Orthodox Christianity
         b. Alexander Nevsky

II. Recovery and Reform of the Catholic Church
   A. Problems of Decline
   B. Cluniac Reform Movement
      1. Duke William's Abbey at Cluny
      2. Spread of the Cluniac Spirit
   C. Reform of the Papacy: Gregory VII and the Investiture Controversy
      1. Pope as Christ's Vicar on Earth
      2. Conflicts with Henry IV
      3. Excommunication
      4. Confrontation at Canossa
      5. Concordat of Worms

III. Christianity and Medieval Civilization
    A.   Growth of the Papal Monarchy
        1.   Centralization of Administration
        2.   Innocent III and the Two Great Lights
    B.   New Religious Orders and Spiritual Ideals
        1.   Cistercians
            a.   Activism
            b.   Bernard of Clairvaux
        2.   Women's Orders: Hildegard of Bingen
        3.   Living the Gospel Life
            a.   Francis of Assisi and Poverty
            b.   Dominic and the Preachers
        4.   Monasticism and Social Services
    C.   Popular Religion in the High Middle Ages
        1.   Sacraments
        2.   Saints
        3.   The Virgin
        4.   Relics
        5.   Indulgences
        6.   Pilgrimages
    D.   Voices of Protest and Intolerance
        1.   Catharism: The Albigensians
        2.   Crusades against Heretics
        3.   The "Holy Office" of Inquisition
        4.   Persecution of the Jews
        5.   Intolerance of Homosexuality

IV. The Crusades
    A.   Background to the Crusades
        1.   Islam and the Seljuk Turks
        2.   Byzantine Empire
            a.   Schism between the Catholic and Orthodox Churches
            b.   The Comneni
    B.   Early Crusades
        1.   Urban II at Clermont
        2.   "Crusade of the Poor"
        3.   First Crusade
            a.   Capture of Jerusalem
            b.   Crusader States of Palestine
    C.   Bernard of Clairvaux and the Second Crusade
    D.   Third Crusade
        1.   Saladin's Successes
        2.   "Crusade of Kings"
    E.   Crusades of the Thirteenth Century
        1.   Sack of Constantinople
        2.   "Children's Crusade"
        3.   Frederick II
        4.   Saint Louis IX
    F.   Effects of the Crusades
        1.   Economic Growth
        2.   Attacks on Muslims and Jews

Chapter Summary

The High Middle Ages saw the growth of European cities and the rise of strong monarchies. The cities and the aristocracies that ran them played an ever-increasing and significant role in cultural development. In England, France, Spain, the Holy Roman Empire, and even Russia royal families brought political and economic stability.

The Catholic Church, which had declined in power and prestige after Charlemagne, reasserted itself at the turn of the millennium. A succession of popes asserted their authority and reformed Church administration. Monastic reform, begun at Cluny in France, spurred a move toward ecclesiastical renewal and purification. Women religious leaders, such as Hildegard of Bingen, added to the spirit of reform. Religion reached down to the peasants, giving them saints to emulate and shrines to visit, preachers to teach them and sacraments to console them.

With the reign of Innocent III (1198-1216) the Church reached the zenith of its influence. At times its zeal to purify society turned mean and led to the persecution of religious groups like the Albigensians and the Jews and of social groups like homosexuals. Out of this ferment came the Crusades. Byzantine rulers called upon the West to reclaim the Holy Land from the "infidel" Muslims; and in a series of invasions that lasted two centuries, kings and knights from the West "took the cross" to "liberate" Palestine. In the end the Crusades were a failure, since all of the land won was eventually reclaimed by the Muslims; but the Crusades did weaken Byzantium, they did strengthen the West, and they led to exploratory journeys and discoveries that took Western culture to the entire world.

Learning Objectives

1. Be able to compare the growth of the English and French monarchies during the High Middle Ages and show how each molded the character of the nation.

2. Be able to trace the Christian re-conquest of the Iberian Peninsula and the kind of social and religious system that it produced.

3. Be able to explain the reasons for the decline and recovery of the Catholic Church in the High Middle Ages, and the part the papacy played in the recovery.

4. Be able to describe popular religion in this period of time, how it affected monastic reform and everyday life, and its relationship to intolerance and persecution.

5. Be able to explain the motivations, achievements, failures, and consequences for European society and world history of the Crusades.

Glossary of Names and Terms

1. Thomas Becket: Archbishop of Canterbury who opposed Henry II's attempt to control the Catholic Church in England and was assassinated by royal agents.

2. Magna Carta: a list of feudal liberties which the English barons forced King John to sign at Runnymede, the first document to limit royal power.

3. Louis IX: King of France who led an exemplary life and a Crusade and was later proclaimed a saint by the Catholic Church.

4.   Alfonso X: King of Castile who called himself "King of Three Religions" and encouraged the development of a cosmopolitan culture shared by Christians, Jews, and Muslims.

5.   Investiture: a lord's act of "investing" a vassal with the symbols of his grant, which became a controversial issue when Pope Gregory VII said laymen could no longer invest Church leaders.

6.   Innocent III: the most powerful of medieval Popes, he declared that he was the sun while the king was the moon.

7.   Cistercians: a reform order of monks who emphasized strict adherence to monastic rules and active resistance to evil.

8.   Hildegard of Bingen: the most distinguished of medieval abbesses, she wrote vivid accounts of her mystical experiences and gave spiritual advice to clerical and lay leaders.

9.   Indulgence: a grant of remission of sins, issued by the Church for charitable deed and contributions and for viewing holy relics.

10. Cathars: declared heretics for their belief that all material things are evil, including the Church, they were hounded to extinction.

Match the Following Words with their Definitions

1.   Plantagenets

2.   Becket

3.   Alexander Nevsky

4.   Cluny

5.   Investiture

6.   Bernard

7.   Hildegard

8.   Urban II

9.   Saladin

10. Louis IX

A.   Ideal example of a Cistercian

B.   English Royal family

C.   Prestigious abbess

D. Preached the First Crusade

E. Repelled German invaders

F. Installation of Church officials

G. Murdered archbishop

H. Led last two crusades

I. Birthplace of reform

J. Let Christians visit holy places

Choose the Correct Answer

1. The landholdings in William of Normandy's England are preserved in

    a. The King's *Royal Register*
    b. John's *Magna Carta*
    c. Bede's *Ecclesiastical History*
    d. Henry I's *Personal Diary*
    e. The *Domesday Book*

2. The Capetians

    a. Survived as rulers due to good fortune and Church support
    b. Ruled Spain with distinction from 1015 to 1350
    c. Died out because they failed to produce heirs
    d. Held their nobility in firm control throughout the Middle Ages
    e. Failed in several attempts to conquer England

3. The French monarchy during the thirteenth century

    a. Suffered humiliating defeats at the hands of England's King John
    b. Was damaged by the scandalous escapades of Louis IX
    c. Encouraged Christians, Muslims, and Jews to support Alfonso X
    d. Inaugurated the Estates-General, the French version of Parliament
    e. Welcomed Jews escaping persecution in Spain

4. One of the most important factors in France's rise to major power status was

    a. The capture of Normandy from the English crown
    b. Subjection to the royal will of the Catholic Church
    c. The popular outpouring of support when democratic reforms were introduced
    d. The decline of Spain and its decision not to challenge its neighbors
    e. Leadership in the Crusades

5. The Christian reconquest of Spain in the thirteenth century

    a. Brought economic prosperity, especially to Andalusia
    b. Completely unified the Iberian Peninsula
    c. Witnessed the expulsion of all Jews and Muslims by Alfonso X
    d. Left Granada the last Muslim kingdom in Iberia
    e. Led to the reconquest of Italy by Vikings

6. Frederick I's dream was to build a

    a. Pleasure palace at Salzburg
    b. Great German Empire with an Italian wing
    c. "Holy Empire" centered in Italy
    d. War machine that would conquer Russia
    e. Temple to Louis IX in Jerusalem

7. The Hohenstaufen ruler Frederick II

    a. Laid the foundations for a strong centralized German monarchy
    b. Created in Sicily the best organized state in Europe
    c. Paid little interest to his Italian possessions
    d. Crushed the power of the German electors
    e. Died in his siege of Jerusalem

8. According to the account of Salimbene de Adam, Frederick II

    a. Was a holy man who prayed five times each day
    b. Often took curiosity to extremes
    c. Cared little for his own physical comfort
    d. Took great care never to contradict Church dogma
    e. Could have been a Scholastic philosopher

9. The Mongols in the thirteenth century

    a. Spread their language to most of Eastern Europe
    b. Conquered almost all of Europe but left of their own accord
    c. Were never once defeated in battle
    d. Contributed administrative skills to backward European states
    e. Entered Europe not to establish permanent rule but for plunder

10. The Mongol invasions of Eastern Europe and Russia led to

    a. The ascendancy of Alexander Nevsky's descendants in Russia
    b. A Muslim cultural legacy throughout Europe
    c. The final destruction of the Mongolian Empire after 1241
    d. The decline of the Russian Orthodox Church
    e. Widespread famine throughout the region

11. The final result of the Investiture Controversy was

    a. The pope's right to consecrate emperors
    b. To ensure that there would be more church-state confrontations in the future
    c. Gregory VII's triumph and empowerment to appoint all clergy
    d. The emperor's right to appoint bishops
    e. Henry VI's excommunication in 1077

12. The abbot of Cluny and the Cluniac reform movement

    a. Reintroduced hard, physical labor to monastic life
    b. Frowned on communal worship, stressing individuality
    c. Decentralized monastic authority to make the houses virtually independent
    d. Left it to the individual monk to decide his moral code
    e. Required monks to train as medical doctors

13. The Cistercians

    a. Showed little growth as a monastic Order in the eleventh century
    b. Eliminated all decoration from monastic buildings
    c. Practiced extreme asceticism and isolation from the world
    d. Comprised a loose alliance of feuding abbeys
    e. Rejected all of Saint Benedict's *Rule*

14. Female monasticism in the twelfth century

    a. Was a completely new Christian phenomenon
    b. Was a refuge for women of all classes
    c. Sharply declined due to a drop in the female birth rate
    d. Had its strongest intellectual tradition in Germany
    e. Led to fears women might someday rule the Church

15. Hildegard of Bingen typified female monasticism in that she

    a. Exercised powers previously reserved for priests
    b. Preached the Sixth Crusade
    c. Was considered by church leaders inferior to male contemplatives
    d. Came from an upper-class background
    e. Lost the respect of most leaders in her old age

16. Francis of Assisi taught his followers to

    a. Obey the wishes of the pope
    b. Grow crops to feed the poor
    c. Live in complete poverty
    d. Go as missionaries to pagan countries
    e. Follow Christ in martyrdom

17. The sacramental system of the Catholic Church

    a.   Was not clearly defined until the fifteenth century
    b.   Made the church an integral part of the individual's life from birth to death
    c.   Was deemed unnecessary for salvation by the Fourth Lateran Council in 1215
    d.   Made the weekly reception of the eucharist a matter of life and death for all Christians
    e.   Was too complicated for the average person to understand

18. Which of the following statements best applies to religion in the High Middle Ages?

    a.   Pilgrimages to holy shrines declined as the sale of indulgences increased
    b.   The Bible was translated and widely read in the vernacular languages
    c.   Popular interest in saints, relics, and pilgrimages led to the building of great shrines
    d.   Priests began distributing printed sermons to their people
    e.   Muslims and Jews in great numbers voluntarily converted to Christianity

19. At the Council of Clermont in 1095, Pope Urban II

    a.   Promised remission of sins to all who would go on a Crusade
    b.   Appointed Peter the Hermit leader of the First Crusade
    c.   Urged the destruction of Jewish settlements along the way to the Holy Land
    d.   Carefully warned of the dangers involved in going on crusades
    e.   Said that he would personally lead a crusade

20. Which of the following statements best describes the first three crusades?

    a.   Only the second one gained permanent victories
    b.   They immediately led to a revival of trade across the continent of Europe
    c.   They had little long-term impact on the nature of European monarchy
    d.   They were all complete failures
    e.   They demonstrated the dangers of joining cross and sword

Complete the Following Sentences

1. At Hastings Duke _____ of _____ defeated the Anglo-Saxon _____ _____ to become King of England.

2. King John of England was forced to sign the _____ _____ when he was captured by his barons at _____.

3. The English parliament grew out of the king's _____ _____ and after 1295 was composed of two _____ from each county and two _____ from each town.

4. Alfonso X of Castile bragged that he was "King of Three Religions," having subjects who were _____, _____, and _____.

5. Alexander Nevsky of _____ allied himself with the _____, defeated the invading _____, and fathered the future princes of _____.

6. In 1075 Pope _____ challenged the right of Emperor _____ to _____ bishops with symbols of their spiritual power.

7. Innocent III compared himself as spiritual ruler to the _____, while comparing kings to the _____, thus making him the _____ power.

8. The holy life of Saint Francis inspired his female admirer, _____, to found a religious Order for women, the _____ _____, who followed his call for lives of _____.

9. The Cathars, whose name means _____, believed in two creators of the world, the God of _____ and Satan, the prince of _____.

10. The zeal to root out heresies led also to the persecution of _____ and _____.

Place the Following in Chronological Order and Give Dates

1. Mongols conquer Russia   1.

2. Thomas Becket is murdered   2.

3. Battle of Hastings   3.

4. French Estates-General meets for the first time   4.

5. First Crusade   5.

6. *Magna Carta* is signed   6.

7. Crusades end   7.

Questions for Critical Thought

1. How did Henry II of England succeed and how did he fail in his drive to be a strong leader? Use the Becket controversy to illustrate both Henry's strengths and weaknesses.

2. What were the short and long term effects for Western Europe of the Christian reconquest of the Iberian Peninsula?

3. Explain the term "Holy Roman Empire," and describe the role it was meant to play and the role it actually played in medieval history.

4. Recount the story of the Investiture Controversy. Why did this confrontation come about, and what were its short and long term results?

5. Explain the ideals of the Cistercian monks. What conditions gave rise to the White Monks, and what contributions did they make to the Church as a whole?

111

6. Explain the appeal to medieval people of relics and pilgrimages. How were their collecting and travelling similar to and different from those of people today?

7. Discuss the place and work of the Franciscans and Dominicans in the world of the High Middle Ages. Why were these Orders needed, and what did they accomplish?

8. Discuss the causes and effects, short and long term, of the Crusades. In what sense did they end the medieval world and bring in the modern age?

Analysis of Primary Source Documents

1. What rights did King John grant to his noble lords in the *Magna Carta*? Show how these rights could, and would much later, be used to claim rights for other classes in England.

2. Given that Salimbene de Adam is a biased witness, show how his accounts still confirm that Frederick II was indeed a twisted genius.

3. What powers did the Pope claim in 1075? Why would a spiritual leader need or even want such powers?

4. Describe the miracle attributed to Saint Bernard. In addition to demonstrating his saintliness, what other themes are illuminated in the story?

5. What does the passage from Hildegard's *Book of Divine Works* tell you about her particular kind of genius? Speculate on the role this woman would play in today's world.

6. What was the typical Christian opinion of Jews in the High Middle Ages? How were such opinions form, and what were the results, both for Christians and for Jews?

7. What methods did Pope Urban II use to persuade Church leaders to launch the First Crusade? Given his persuasive skills, what position would you give him in a modern corporation?

8. By combining the two accounts of the fall of Jerusalem to the crusaders, draw as objective a picture as possible of what happened that day.

CHAPTER 11
THE LATER MIDDLE AGES:
CRISIS AND DISINTEGRATION IN
THE FOURTEENTH CENTURY

Chapter Outline

I.   Time of Troubles: Black Death and Social Crisis
    A.   Famine and Population
    B.   Black Death
        1.   *Yersinium Pestis*
        2.   Mongol Migrations
        3.   Devastation and Depopulation
        4.   Reactions to the Plague
            a.   Flagellants
            b.   Anti-Semitism
    C.   Economic Dislocation and Social Upheaval
        1.   Noble Landlords and Peasants
        2.   Rural Revolts
            a.   *Jacquerie* in France
            b.   Peasant Revolt in England
        3.   City Revolts

II. War and Political Instability
    A.   Causes of the Hundred Years' War
        1.   English King's Claim to France
        2.   Seizure of Gascony by the French Crown
    B.   Conduct and Course of the War
        1.   English Bowmen Defeat French at Crécy
        2.   French King Captured at Poitiers
        3.   English Victory at Agincourt
        4.   Joan of Arc
    C.   Political Instability
        1.   Noble Factions
        2.   Lack of Royal Male Heirs
        3.   Monarchical Insolvency
    D.   Growth of England's Political Institutions
        1.   Parliament: Lords and Commons
        2.   Splintered Royalty
    E.   Problems of the French Kings
        1.   Absence of National Unity
        2.   Taxation
        3.   Insanity of Charles VI
    F.   German Monarchy
        1.   Breakup of the Empire
        2.   Electoral System
    G.   States of Italy: Milan, Florence, and Venice

III. Decline of the Church
    A. Boniface VIII and the Conflict with the State
        1. *Unam Sanctam*
        2. Election of a French Pope
    B. Papacy at Avignon (1305-1377)
        1. Improved Church Administration
        2. Taxes and Splendor
    C. Great Schism (1378-1415)
        1. National Division
        2. Decline in Prestige
    D. New Thoughts on Church and State
        1. Marsiglio of Padua and *Defender of the Peace*
        2. Conciliar Movement
        3. Schism Ended
    E. Popular Religion in an Age of Adversity
        1. Good Works and Family Chapels
        2. Mysticism and Lay Piety
            a. Meister Eckhart
            b. Brothers of the Common Life
        3. Women Mystics
    F. Changes in Theology: William of Occam

IV. Cultural World of the Fourteenth Century
    A. Vernacular Literature
        1. Dante's *Divine Comedy*
        2. Petrarch's Sonnets to Laura
        3. Boccaccio's *Decameron*
        4. Chaucer's *Canterbury Tales*
        5. Christine de Pizan's *Book of the City of Ladies*
    B. Art and the Black Death: Giotto's Realism

V. Society in an Age of Adversity
    A. Changes in Urban Life
        1. Brothels
        2. Family Life and Gender Roles
        3. Medieval Children
    B. New Directions in Medicine
        1. Medical Schools
        2. "Four Humors"
        3. Surgeons
        4. Public Health and Sanitation
    C. Inventions and New Patterns
        1. Mechanical Clocks
        2. Eyeglasses
        3. Gunpowder

Chapter Summary

After the grand adventures of the twelfth and thirteenth centuries, the crises and social disintegration of the fourteenth century shocked the whole of Europe. Economic, social, military, political, religious, and even intellectual and cultural crises led to a sense of desperation and doom. As in every age, some people surrendered to pessimism; as in every age, some took the chaos as a challenge, endured it, and eventually triumphed over it.

The economic and social crises were caused by famine, plague, and fumbling attempts to adjust to new realities in rural and urban life. There were revolts both in the countryside and in the growing cities, all of them born of desperation, all seeking redress of grievances in a world that appeared less and less just. The Hundred Years' War between England and France affected all of Europe and led to military and political instability.

The decline in the power of the triumphal Church of the previous century began with the claim of Pope Boniface VIII to temporal supremacy and a challenge to his claim from Philip IV of France. When their feud was over, the papacy was forcibly moved to Avignon and remained there for most of a century; and after that there came a schism that rent the church for another quarter century. Yet while church leaders began calling for a change in ecclesiastical structure, with power devolving to councils, religion among the masses remained strong, and a mystical movement swept the monasteries.

Even the unity of Scholastic thought and Latin literature seemed to be crumbling. Late Scholasticism challenged its own firm foundations, and poets began more and more to write in their vernacular languages. On the other hand, urban life adjusted to new times, as it must, and there were advances in medical and technological fields. Instability and chaos slowed but did not derail human development.

Learning Objectives

1. Be able to explain the causes and both the short and long term effects on European religion and society of the Black Death.

2. Be able to explain the causes of the Hundred Years' War, to describe its turning points, and to account for its outcome.

3. Be able to describe how and why the governments of England, France, and the German lands changed in the late Middle Ages.

4. Be able to explain the reasons for the decline in the power of the Church in the fourteenth century and how religious leaders responded.

5. Be able to show the effects that social upheaval and ecclesiastical decline had on culture, particularly popular religion and literature, in the fourteenth century.

Glossary of Names and Terms

1. *Yersinia pestis*: deadly bacterium carried by fleas which brought the Black Death or Bubonic Plague and its resulting horrors to Western Europe in 1347.

2. *Jacquerie*: the peasant revolt, brought about by the plague and its economic dislocation, which swept through France in 1358.

3. Wat Tyler: leader of the Peasants' Revolt in England in 1381, which forced the government to withdraw the poll tax.

4. Agincourt: site of the battle in 1415 where England's Henry V defeated the French army and won the right to inherit the French throne.

5. Joan of Arc: peasant girl who believed she had a divine commission to save France from the English and inspired the French victory in the Hundred Years' War.

6. *Unam Sanctam*: the pronouncement by Pope Boniface VIII that he held power over all secular rulers which led to his capture and death.

7. Conciliarism: movement responding to the decline in papal prestige that advocated the right of councils to make Church policy.

8. Meister Eckhart: German Dominican theologian who encouraged the growth of popular religion by proclaiming the mystical union of man's soul with God.

9. Dante: Florentine poet whose *Comedy* vividly portrayed the political and theological world of the Late Middle Ages.

10. Chaucer: English poet whose *Canterbury Tales* not only captured British life in the fourteenth century but contributed to the development of the English language.

Match the Following Words with their Definitions

1. Pogrom

2. Jacquerie

3. Wat Tyler

4. Agincourt

5. Avignon

6. Conciliarism

7. Gerard Groote

8. Nominalism

9. Dante

10. Giotto

A.   Author who bridged the Middle Ages and the Renaissance

B.   Persecution of Jews

C.   Painter whose realism foreshadowed Renaissance art
D.   Site of the greatest English victory of the Hundred Years' War

E.   Founder of Modern Devotion

F.   Leader of the Peasants' Revolt

G.   Revolt of French townspeople against monarchical power

H.   Movement to take power from a corrupt papacy

I.   Site of the papal court, 1305-78

J.   Challenge to Scholastic assumptions

Choose the Correct Answer

1.   The Black Death of 1348-1350

   a.   Was one of many plagues to hit Europe between the eighth and fourteenth centuries
   b.   Started in northern and moved to southern Europe
   c.   Recurred in outbreaks throughout the fourteenth and fifteenth centuries
   d.   Ended as quickly as it began
   e.   Never reached England or Scandinavia

2.   The flagellants

   a.   Carried battle flags for the armies of the French kings
   b.   Abused themselves in order to win God's forgiveness
   c.   Treated victims of the Black Death with experimental medical procedures
   d.   Were commended by several popes for their service
   e.   Were declared heretics during in the late fourteenth century

3.   The persecutions of Jews during the time of the Black Death

   a.   Were instigated by the Catholic clergy
   b.   Led to the execution of nearly all Jews in Poland
   c.   Reached their worst limits in German cities
   d.   Had little to do with economics and finance
   e.   Were unusual in the history of Christian-Jewish relations

4.   The French movement known as the *Jacquerie*

   a.   Had no particular political agenda
   b.   Was in part caused by the upheavals of the Black Death and the Hundred Years' War
   c.   Ended with a peasant victory in certain regions of the country
   d.   Was led completely by farmers
   e.   Had no influence outside France itself

5. The English peasants' revolt of 1381 differed from other such revolts in that it

    a. Was caused by rising economic expectations
    b. Was brutally crushed by the nobility
    c. Succeeded in getting the government to agree to its plans
    d. Gained long-term benefits for the peasants
    e. Had largely clerical leadership

6. The Hundred Years' War was characterized by

    a. Early English losses to the French army
    b. England's refusal to consider using new military weapons
    c. English raids on defenseless villages
    d. Strong French royal leadership
    e. Papal preference for the English over the French

7. Among the general trends of fourteenth-century European politics was

    a. Parliaments founded in many countries
    b. Chronic financial shortfalls among rulers
    c. The end of factionalized nobility
    d. The stability of traditional feudal loyalties
    e. Mystical devotion by most rulers

8. In the fourteenth century France saw

    a. The increasing dominance of the Estates-General
    b. No new forms of government revenues
    c. Near civil war over monarchial succession
    d. All classes represented in government
    e. Victory over the English in the Hundred Years' War

9. The German Golden Bull of 1356

    a. Made Charles IV the first in a line of hereditary rulers
    b. Ensured the independence of ecclesiastical states
    c. Placed all religious leaders under the direct command of the emperor
    d. Ensured strong central government for a century
    e. Gave seven electors the power to choose the "King of the Romans"

10. Pope Boniface VIII

    a. Reasserted papal supremacy with great success
    b. Never challenged the temporal power of kings
    c. Fought with Edward I of England over whether clergy should pay taxes
    d. Died in 1305 when captured by Philip IV
    e. Was soon after his death proclaimed a saint

11. At Avignon the papacy

    a. Made its bureaucracy more specialized and efficient
    b. Gained prestige throughout Europe
    c. Suffered from lack of income
    d. Became a more purely spiritual institution
    e. Developed a more efficient method of papal succession

12. From 1378 to 1417 the Church experienced a

    a. Revival of mysticism and intellectual ferment
    b. Schism and loss of popular confidence
    c. Reunification of formerly hostile factions
    d. Moral reformation and increase in monastic volunteers
    e. Growth in royal support across the continent

13. One result of the Great Schism was to

    a. Put an end to ecclesiastical financial abuses
    b. Make Christians doubt the spiritual authority of the Church
    c. Rejuvenate Christianity after a spiritual decline
    d. Make the pope a stronger figure
    e. Increase the power of England in ecclesiastical affairs

14. Marsiglio of Padua, in his *Defender of the Peace*,

    a. Argued for the right of the pope to intervene in secular affairs
    b. Supported Clement VIII over Urban VI in the Great Schism
    c. Claimed that all spiritual authority lay with the pope
    d. Argued that councils should make church policy
    e. Said all Europeans should recognize the German Emperor as overlord

15. Fourteenth-century mysticism

    a. Was inspired by nominalist philosophy
    b. Found its greatest response in France and Italy
    c. Emphasized the union of the human soul with God
    d. Was fully endorsed and controlled by the papacy
    e. Found support only among the upper classes

16. Identify the correct description among these mystics

    a. Gerhard Groote---most influential of Swiss mystics
    b. Richard Rolle---founder of the Brothers of the Common Life
    c. Johannes Tauler---author of the Modern Devotion
    d. Meister Eckhart---sparked the mystical movement in western Germany
    e. Catherine of Siena---founder of the Sisters of the Common Life

17. Dante's *Divine Comedy*

    a. Described the soul's progression to salvation
    b. Was the last literary work written in Latin
    c. Lashed out at the classics as barbarous
    d. Attacked the science of Aristotle
    e. Carefully avoided any political commentary

18. The Florentine writer Petrarch is known for all of the following *except*

    a. Sonnets written in the Italian vernacular
    b. A call for the revival of classical learning
    c. A book of folk tales called the *Decameron*
    d. Strong advocacy of individualism
    e. Sonnets to a woman named Laura

19. New directions in medicine during the fourteenth century included

    a. The rise of surgeons to greater prominence
    b. More training courses in medical techniques
    c. An increase in the number and accessibility of medical textbooks
    d. Municipal boards of health
    e. All of the above

20. Giovanni di Dondi's clock

    a. Showed the signs of the zodiac
    b. Could be found in every royal court throughout Europe
    c. Was easily constructed and soon became widely owned
    d. Was the first mechanical instrument to be patented
    e. Proved too unreliable to be of use to armies

Complete the Following Sentence

1. The Black Death is believed to have come to Europe from _____, carried by _____. It is believed to have killed between ____ and _____ percent of Europe's population.

2. The Peasants' Revolt in England, led by the farmer ____ _____ and the preacher _____ _____, did at least bring an end to the hated _____ ____.

3. While the English defeated the French at _____ in 1356 and at _____ in 1415, the Hundred Years' War ended in 1453 with England holding only the port of _____.

4. According to the Golden Bull of 1356, the _____ would henceforth be elected by _____ lay and _____ ecclesiastical princes.

5. When Boniface VIII declared his temporal supremacy in _____ _____, Philip IV took the pope prisoner at _____ and forced the next pope to settle in the French city of _____.

6. The Great Schism led to a movement outlined by _____ of _____ called _____. He referred to the Church as a _____ of the _____.

7. Late medieval mysticism affected all kinds of people, from Dominican theologian _____ _____ to canon lawyer _____ _____ and inspired schools led by Brothers and Sisters of the _____ _____.

8. In Dante's *Divine Comedy* the classical author _____ represented human reason, the woman _____ represented revelation, and _____ _____ represented mystical contemplation.

9. Chaucer gave the English language dignity by using it to write his _____ _____, the story of pilgrims on their way from _____ outside London to the shrine of _____ _____.

10. Late medieval physicians believed that good health came from a balance of the body's four _____. Cures for illnesses included _____ medicines and _____.

Place the Following in Chronological Order and Give Dates:

1. Great Schism begins   1.

2. Hundred Years' War ends   2.

3. Joan of Arc leads French army   3.

4. French Jacquerie crushed   4.

5. *Unam Sanctam* issued   5.

6. Hundred Years' War begins   6.

7. Battle of Agincourt   7.

Questions for Critical Thought

1. Discuss the causes of the Black Death and its effects on late medieval society, particularly the economic dislocation and social upheaval that followed it.

2. What caused the peasant revolts in the fourteenth century? What forms did they take in various countries? What did they achieve?

3. What were the immediate causes of the Hundred Years' War? What were the stakes for the French and the English?

4. What caused movements toward democracy in France to fail while such efforts in England made some progress?

5. Show how the Golden Bull of 1356 A.D. established both the independence of the Holy Roman Empire without modernizing the state.

6.   What caused the Great Schism, and what effects did it have on late medieval religious life? How did the average Christian carry on his/her religious devotions during the period when the church was in such a state of chaos?

7.   Define mysticism. Give examples of how it entered late medieval religious life and of what effects it had both on the Church and on society.

8.   Why did late medieval writers begin to use their vernacular languages? What did Western civilization lose and what did it gain by their doing so?

Analysis of Primary Source Documents

1.   Describe the effects of the Black Death on individuals and cities. Why was it attributed to the wrath of God?

2.   Explain how superstition, fear, prejudice, and greed combined to cause the attack upon European Jews in 1349.

3.   Describe the actions of French peasants during the *Jacquerie*. What does their violence tell you about the conditions under which they had been forced to live and how they themselves had been treated by their masters?

4.   Using the town of Limoges as your example, describe the treatment of civilians during the Hundred Years' War.

5.   What kind of language does Catherine de Pizan use to portray Joan of Arc both as a heroic soldier and the essence of womanhood? How does she achieve her goal of making the French war of liberation from the English seem to be a holy cause?

6.   Summarize the claims Pope Boniface VIII made for papal authority in *Unam Sanctam*. What does the fact that this declaration caused such violent reaction say about prior understandings of papal power?

7.   Dante believed that a person's sin on earth meets with appropriate punishment in the world to come. How does the passage you have read from his "Inferno" illustrate this point?

8.   What does the legal assumption that women are without rights say about the philosophical and anthropological assumptions of late medieval society?

CHAPTER 12
RECOVERY AND REBIRTH:
THE AGE OF THE RENAISSANCE

Chapter Outline

I. Meaning and Characteristics of the Renaissance
    A. Urban Society
    B. Age of Recovery
    C. Rebirth of Classical Culture
    D. Recovery of the Individual

II. Making of Renaissance Society
    A. Economic Recovery
        1. Hanseatic League
        2. Wool and Silk
        3. Banking and the Medici
    B. Social Changes
        1. Domination of the Nobility
        2. Courtly Society in Castiglione's *Courtier*
        3. Peasants and Townspeople
        4. Slavery
    C. Family in Renaissance Italy
        1. Marriage
        2. Children
        3. Sexual Norms

III. Italian States in the Renaissance
    A. The Five Major States
    B. Independent City-States
    C. Warfare in Italy
    D. Birth of Modern Diplomacy
    E. Machiavelli and the New Statecraft

IV. Intellectual Renaissance in Italy
    A. Humanism
        1. Emergence and Petrarch
        2. Civil Humanism and Leonardo Bruni
        3. Lorenzo Valla
        4. Ficino and the Platonic Academy
        5. Hermeticism and Pico della Mirandola
    B. Education
        1. Vittorino da Feltre and "the Liberal Studies"
        2. Pietro Paolo Vergerio's *Concerning Character*
    C. Humanism and History
        1. Secularization of History
        2. Francesco Guicciardini
    D. Impact of Printing
        1. Johannes Gutenberg's Bible
        2. Scholarly Research and Lay Readership

V.   The Artistic Renaissance
    A.   Art in the Early Renaissance
        1. Masaccio
        2. Uccello
        3. Botticelli
        4. Donatello
        5. Brunelleschi
        6. Piero della Francesca
    B.   The Artistic High Renaissance
        1. Leonardo da Vinci
        2. Raphael
        3. Michelangelo
        4. Bramante
    C.   Artist and Social Status: Artist as Hero
    D.   Northern Artistic Renaissance
        1. Jan Van Eyck
        2. Albrecht Dürer
    E.   Music in the Renaissance
        1. Dufay
        2. Madrigal

VI. European State in the Renaissance
    A.   Growth of the French Monarchy
        1. Charles VII and the *Taille*
        2. Louis XI and Commerce
    B.   England: Civil War and New Monarchy
        1. War of the Roses
        2. Henry VII and the Tudors
    C.   Unification of Spain
        1. Ferdinand and Isabella
        2. Expulsion of Muslims and Jews
        3. Inquisition
    D.   Holy Roman Empire: Success of the Habsburgs
    E.   Struggle for Strong Monarchy in Eastern Europe
    F.   Ottoman Turks and the End of Byzantium

VII. Church in the Renaissance
    A.   Heresy and Reform
        1. John Wyclif's Lollards
        2. John Hus
        3. The Doctrine of *Sacrosancta*
        4. Pius II and *Execrabilis*
    B.   Renaissance Papacy
        1. Sixtus IV and Alexander VI
        2. Julius II and the New Saint Peter's
        3. Leo X and Raphael

Chapter Summary

The Age of the Renaissance has a distinct image in most people's minds. It is one of our most recognized eras, populated with artists and writers of great genius, vivid imagination, and amazing skill. They looked back to the Greeks and Romans for their inspiration, and they looked forward as they created the modern world. Yet the violence of its rising political leaders and daring of its financiers made it, as one historian has said, an age characterized by "the mixed scent of blood and roses."

The strong economic recovery of the day, prefiguring the modern world, created a refined courtly society which supported the arts but planted seeds of envy in the hearts of peasants and city laborers who did not share the wealth. Strong Italian merchants and European kings held seats of power. Writers and artists, widely honored for their work, served at the pleasure and taste of wealthy patrons. Renaissance popes, freeing themselves from the fourteenth century's chaos, used their office to enrich themselves and their families. Heresy loomed, and intellectuals called for reform.

Still the roll call of personalities—Castiglione, Machiavelli, Ficino, Pico, Leonardo, Michelangelo, Raphael—confirms that the Renaissance was indeed an age of genius and achievement, a high point in Western Civilization.

Learning Objectives

1. Be able to describe the social changes that characterize Renaissance life, particularly alterations in the economic system, class structure, and family life.

2. Be able to explain the historical events that led to Machiavelli's theories of statecraft and how his theories differed from the published works of political theorists before him.

3. Be able to define Renaissance humanism and show how it reached into all branches of edition, politics, learning, and into the arts.

4. Be able to describe the new forms of art and architecture the Renaissance introduced and sustained, from the early works of Masaccio through those of Raphael.

5. Be able to detail the character of the Renaissance Papacy and Church, how it developed skills that enabled it to survive a difficult era yet developed characteristics that called for reform.

Glossary of Names and Terms

1. Jacob Burckhardt: Swiss historian of the nineteenth century who started the modern study of the Renaissance as a distinct period.

2. Medici: Florentine banking family that became not only rulers of the city but the greatest patrons of Renaissance art.

3. Isabella d'Este: one of the Renaissance's most impressive women, often called "first lady of the world," whose court in Mantua attracted artists and writers.

4. *The Prince*: short work by Machiavelli which outlined the characteristics that could establish a leader and make him successful, all without personal moral integrity.

5. Vittorino da Feltre: founder of a school in Mantua, where he based the curriculum on classical "liberal studies" and set the standard for humanistic education.

6. Johannes Gutenberg: pioneer of the use of moveable metal type for printing, whose Bible of 1456 was the first book in the Western world produced with the new method.

7. Masaccio: artist whose series of frescoes in Florence is considered to be the first great masterpiece of Early Renaissance art, establishing a style that endured.

8. John Wyclif: Oxford theologian who was the first reformer to condemn Church corruption and call for popes to be stripped of authority and power.

9. Nepotism: derived from the Greek word for nephew, the word was coined to describe the awarding of offices, particularly Church commissions, to relatives.

10. Julius II: pope who led his army into battle and whose artistic patronage included raising money to build the new Saint Peter's in Rome.

Match the Following Words with their Definitions

1. Castiglione

2. Machiavelli

3. Leonardo Bruni

4. Marsilio Ficino

5. Pico della Mirandola

6. Michelangelo

7. Charles VII

8. Henry VII

9. Julius II

10. Leo X

A. Founder of Florence's Platonic Academy

B. Called even in his day "Il Divino"

C. Established the Court of the Star Chamber

D. Renaissance authority on courtly etiquette

E. Warrior pope who decided to rebuild Saint Peter's Church

F.   Advocate of Ciceronian civil humanism

G.   Medici pope who commissioned Raphael to paint frescoes in the Vatican

H.   Humanist who called Hermetic philosophy the "science of the Divine"

I.   Author of the "realistic" Renaissance treatise on politics

J.   Established the French royal army

Choose the Correct Answer:

1.   The Italian Renaissance

   a.   Was born in the universities
   b.   Saw a spiritual renewal within the papacy
   c.   Transformed rural life
   d.   Demonstrated that Europe was recovering from the fourteenth century's calamities
   e.   Saw little economic change in the cities

2.   Economic developments in the Renaissance included

   a.   The concentration of wealth in fewer hands
   b.   Increased employment as wool gave way to luxury goods
   c.   An economic boom that rivaled that of the thirteenth century
   d.   New trade opened between Italy and the Ottoman Turks
   e.   A papacy that needed less and less support from bankers

3.   Castiglione's *Courtier*

   a.   Rejected the idea of a classical education
   b.   Outlined the rules of aristocratic society
   c.   Advocated Hedonistic pursuits
   d.   Disapproved of the active political life
   e.   Described how to be selected pope

4.   Renaissance banquets were

   a.   Simpler and more informal than those of the Middle Ages
   b.   Never held on Holy Days or Sabbaths
   c.   Used to demonstrate power and wealth
   d.   Banned from the Vatican after 1417
   e.   Used primarily to celebrate baptisms and weddings

5.   The "third estate" of the fifteenth century was

   a.   Predominantly urban and commercial
   b.   Essentially free of the manorial system
   c.   Relatively free from the old menaces of violence and disease
   d.   Almost a thing of the past
   e.   Highly stratified, both socially and economically

6. The reintroduction of slavery in the fourteenth century occurred largely as a result of

    a. The capture of Slavic prisoners of war
    b. The shortage of labor caused by the Black Death
    c. Papal decrees calling for a paternal relationship between nobles and peasants
    d. Feelings of Italian racial superiority
    e. Any alternatives to deal with Muslims and Jews

7. Which of the following statements was *not* true of Renaissance Italian society?

    a. A strong family bond provided political and economic security in a violent world
    b. Prostitution was considered a necessary evil
    c. Dowries were measures of upward and downward mobility
    d. The father had total power over the children
    e. Women had power only as managers of the household

8. Machiavelli's *Prince* paved the way for

    a. Republican government in many Italian cities
    b. Higher moral standards for Renaissance politicians
    c. The modern secular concept of power politics
    d. Higher moral standards in the papacy
    e. None of the above

9. Petrarch affected Renaissance humanism by encouraging all of the following *except*

    a. A more rational approach to the veneration of saintly relics
    b. The use of Ciceronian Latin for poetry and prose
    c. The dismissal of the time just preceding his own as a "dark" age
    d. A search for ancient manuscripts
    e. A deeply spiritual approach to life while pursuing classical ideals

10. Marsilio Ficino sought in his writings to

    a. Synthesize Christian theology and Platonic philosophy
    b. Explain the characteristics of good political leadership
    c. Revive the flagging mysticism of his day
    d. Prove to the Medici that he would be a valuable secretary
    e. Describe proper courtly behavior

11. Pico della Mirandola's *Oration* stated that humans are

    a. Fallen creatures but can regain paradise through public service
    b. Nothing more than amoral beasts
    c. Divine and destined for eternal glory
    d. Capable of choosing whether to be earthly or spiritual creatures
    e. Helpless without the sacraments of the Church

12. The educational systems established by Vittorino da Feltre and Pietro Paolo Vergerio

    a. Had as its primary goal the well-rounded citizen
    b. Was designed for rich and poor alike
    c. Concentrated more on science than on verbal skills
    d. Excluded all moral or religious teaching
    e. Gave little emphasis to physical exercise and training

13. The influence of humanism on the writing of history can be seen in the way humanists

    a. Looked for evidence of God's hand in historical events
    b. Emphasized the influence of political, economic, and social forces
    c. So viciously attacked Christianity
    d. Relied on archeology to explain historical mysteries
    e. Rejected the historical accounts of peasants

14. The advent of printing brought about

    a. Disputes over the authenticity of ancient texts
    b. Criticism of the money printers made
    c. A noticeable increase in lay readership
    d. Calls for censorship of pornographic materials
    e. A movement in the papacy to ban heretical titles

15. Italian artists of the fifteenth century

    a. Ignored nature and painted from their "inner light"
    b. Sought to portray naturalism and realism
    c. Often copied the works of fourteenth century artists
    d. Abandoned the study of anatomy
    e. Had little interest in the classical studies of humanists

16. The artist Uccello

    a. Painted the first chapel ceiling
    b. Dissected cadavers in order to learn anatomy
    c. Called for a return to Byzantine styles
    d. Used human figures were mere props to demonstrate space and perspective
    e. Depended on papal patronage to survive

17. The architecture of Brunelleschi was inspired by

    a. His years as a sculptor
    b. Ruins he studied in Rome
    c. Designs borrowed from French Gothic cathedrals
    d. Models of Byzantine churches in Constantinople
    e. The humanistic art of Masaccio

Chapter 12

18. Jan van Eyck's works demonstrate the Northern Renaissance's concern with

    a.   Accurate portrayal of details
    b.   Depiction of papal and royal coronations
    c.   Moral lessons drawn from scenes of debauchery
    d.   Peasant life in holiday festivities
    e.   The works of ancient Greece and Rome

19. Examples of religious unrest in the fifteenth century included

    a.   John Wyclif and the Lollard movement in Germany
    b.   The refusal of England's Henry VII to send a tithe to Rome
    c.   The condemnation and execution of John Hus
    d.   Papal calls for the decrees of *Sacrosancta* and *Frequens*
    e.   The march on Rome by an army of Nepotists

20. The Renaissance pope Sixtus IV is remembered for

    a.   Participating in parades and carnivals
    b.   Using the papacy to increase his family's power and wealth
    c.   Poisoning his enemies
    d.   Having mistresses share his Vatican apartments
    e.   Commissioning Michelangelo to paint the ceiling of his chapel

Complete the Following Sentences

1.   The Florentine family of _____ was rich enough to serve as _____ for the papacy; but their property was confiscated in 1494 by the invading King of _____.

2.   Castiglione, in his *Book of the* _____, outlined the ideal character of and conduct for European _____. They should openly demonstrate their accomplishments but with _____.

3.   Isabella d'Este, educated at her father's court at _____, attracted humanists to her husband's court at _____, where she amassed a famous _____ for humanists to use.

4.   Having lost his position as a diplomat for the Republic of _____, Machiavelli turned his mind to political theory and wrote _____ _____, in which he argued that _____ plays no part in realistic politics.

5.   While _____ is considered Father of the Renaissance, its greatest statement, *Oration on the Dignity of Man*, was authored by _____ _____ _____. In it he held that human potential is _____.

6.   The High Renaissance was dominated by three artistic geniuses, _____, _____, and _____, oldest to youngest.

7.   Bramante, who like Raphael came to Rome from _____, was chosen by Pope _____ to design the new basilica of _____ _____.

8. Michelangelo complained that Northern Renaissance art, though it agreeably impressed the
_____, was without _____ or _____.

9. After their conquest of Grenada, Ferdinand of Aragon and Isabella of Castile in 1492
expelled all _____ who would not convert to Christianity from Spain and in 1502 expelled
all remaining _____ from Castille, thus earning the title _____ _____
monarchs.

10. Renaissance popes had unsavory reputations, particularly the warrior-pope _____,
the pope who made five of his nephews cardinals, _____, and the pope who was
infamous for his debauchery, _____.

Place the Following in Chronological Order and Give Dates

1. Marriage of Ferdinand and Isabella   1.

2. Sack of Rome   2.

3. End of the Great Schism   3.

4. Fall of Constantinople   4.

5. Expulsion of the Spanish Jews   5.

6. Pragmatic Sanction of Bourges   6.

7. Battle of Bosworth Field   7.

Questions for Critical Thought

1. As applied to the early modern period of Western civilization, what does the term
"Renaissance" mean? What areas of life did it affect most?

2. What exactly was the role Castiglione played in the development of Italian courtly society?
Describe his ideal courtier.

3. In what sense can it be said that Machiavelli created a new political science? Describe it.
What message does it have for modern readers?

4. Define Renaissance humanism. What effects did it have on theories and practices of
education.

5. Compare and contrast Italian and Northern styles of Renaissance art. Which is now
considered more universal in appeal? Why?

6. Recount the way in which Spain was united. Explain how different trails to unity might have
made for a different final product, a different Spain.

7. What was the nature of the new heresies of the Renaissance period? How did they differ and how were they like previous ones? How was reaction to them by the church like and unlike reaction to previous ones?

8. Describe the Renaissance papacy by discussing its major figures, their lives, their accomplishments. Had you been a contemporary scholar, what remedies would you have prescribed for the problems of the church under their leadership?

Analysis of Primary Source Documents

1. What conclusions can be drawn about the wealthy Renaissance man's diet and probable health and life expectancy by perusing the menu from one of Pope Pius V's banquets? Do you consider it unseemly for a pope and his guests to enjoy such food? Why or why not?

2. According to the letters of Alessandra Strozzi, what characteristics and advantages did a Renaissance family look for when searching out a wife for one of its sons? What kind of marriage would he likely have?

3. From her letters what do we know of Isabella d'Este as a ruler? Why was she considered such an unusual woman for her times?

4. What was Machiavelli's advice to a prince who wanted to hold power? How did Erasmus describe the Christian prince? Explain why did these contrasting theories about governance stood side by side in the Renaissance.

5. Use Petrarch's *Ascent of Mt. Ventoux* to illustrate what some historians call Renaissance man's dual nature: medieval and modern.

6. Use Pico della Mirandola's *Oration on the Dignity of Man* to demonstrate what the humanists believed man's nature and potential to be.

7. What do the words of Laura Cereta tell you of her attitude toward the man who criticized her for her intellect? What did she think of woman who did not use their own?

8. What qualities made Leonardo an artistic genius in Vasari's estimation? What does Vasari believe is the source of such genius?

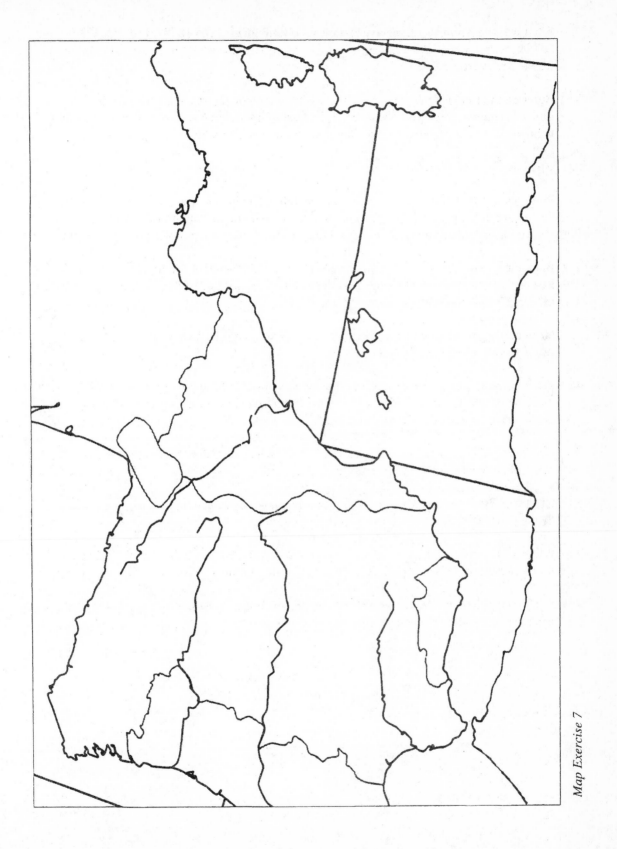

Map Exercise 7

Chapter 12

Map Exercise 7: The Iberian Peninsula in 1479

Shade and label the following

1. Aragon
2. Balearic Islands
3. Castile
4. France
5. Granada
6. Navarre
7. Portugal

Pinpoint and label the following

1. Barcelona
2. Lisbon
3. Madrid
4. Toledo
5. Valencia

CHAPTER 13
REFORMATION AND RELIGIOUS WARFARE IN THE SIXTEENTH CENTURY

Chapter Outline

I.   Prelude to Reformation
     A.   Christian or Northern Renaissance Humanism
          1.   Erasmus
          2.   Thomas More
     B.   Church and Religion on the Eve of the Reformation
          1.   The Search for Salvation
          2.   Calls for Reform
          3.   Influence on the Protestant Revolt

II. Martin Luther and the Reformation in Germany
     A.   Early Luther
          1.   Indulgence Controversy
          2.   The Quickening Rebellion
     B.   Rise of Lutheranism
          1.   Spread of Luther's Ideas
          2.   The Peasant's War

III. Germany and the Reformation: Religion and Politics
     A.   The Ottoman Empire
     B.   Politics in Germany

IV. Spread of the Protestant Reformation
     A.   Lutheranism in Scandinavia
     B.   The Zwinglian Reformation
          1.   Reforms in Zürich
          2.   Futile Search for Unity
     C.   The Radical Reformation: The Anabaptists
          1.   The Ideas of the Anabaptists
          2.   Varieties of Anabaptists
     D.   Reformation in England
          1.   The New Order
          2.   Reaction under Mary
     E.   Calvinism
          1.   Calvin's Ideas
          2.   Calvin's Geneva

V. Social Impact of the Protestant Reformation
    A. Effect on Families
        1. More Positive Attitudes
        2. Place of Women
        3. Home Devotions
    B. Education in the Reformation
        1. Rise of the German Gymnasium
        2. Genevan Academy
    C. Religious Practices and Popular Culture
        1. Decline of "Catholic" Practices among Protestants
        2. Reform of Social Practices and the Rise of Puritanism

VI. Catholic Reformation
    A. Revival of the Old
    B. The Society of Jesus
        1. Activities of the Jesuits
    C. Revived Papacy
    D. The Council of Trent

VII. Politics and the Wars of Religion in the Sixteenth Century
    A. French Wars of Religion (1562-1598)
        1. Course of the Struggle
    B. Philip II and Militant Catholicism
    C. Revolt of the Netherlands
    D. England of Elizabeth
        1. Religious Policy
        2. Foreign Policy
        3. Spanish Armada

Chapter Summary

The great religious earthquake called the Reformation, which split the Church into two and then into a dozen parts, was caused by a variety of social and economic developments. Still it depended upon the Renaissance humanism of its day for an intellectual rationale. Christian humanists, particularly in the north of Europe, led the movement to reform and purify the Catholic Church, even though some of them refused to be Protestants; and it was their writings which gave the Reformation its direction.

The Reformation began with Martin Luther's criticism of the sale of indulgences and his subsequent excommunication. It spread from Germany to Switzerland through the work of John Calvin and Ulrich Zwingli and to Scotland and Holland through the work of Calvin's disciples. Although in England the break with the Catholic Church came because Henry VIII wanted a divorce, the English Reformation grew more radical after Henry's death. Christendom fragmented.

While northern Europe, with the notable exceptions of France, Poland, and Ireland, left the Catholic faith, the southern nations of Italy, Spain, and Portugal, as well as France and Austria, remained firmly Catholic. The Council of Trent, called too late to stop the permanent division, confirmed the Catholic teachings of the Middle Ages while implementing many of the reforms of practice advocated by Luther and Calvin. The Age of Reformation left all of the churches stronger in conviction yet at war with each other over authority.

In France the Catholic establishment tried to wipe out the Protestant minority, the Huguenots, and came to an uneasy peace only with the Edict of Nantes. Philip II, who earned the title "Most Catholic King," blocked all Protestant activity in his Spanish kingdom but lost his Dutch provinces to the Protestant House of Orange and his naval Armada to Protestant England. The English queen Elizabeth presided over the establishment of a national church that included most Englishmen but did not tolerate those who chose a different path.

Learning Objectives

1. Be able to describe the status and character of the Catholic Church just prior to the outbreak of the Reformation, and show how such things contributed to the breakup of Christianity.

2. Be able to outline the major points of contention between Martin Luther and the Church, and show why they did not find a way to compromise and avoid schism.

3. Be able to discuss the various forms Protestantism took and how these groups became dominant in various parts of Europe.

4. Be able to examine the social and economic impact of the Reformation and Protestantism on the continent of Europe.

5. Be able to describe the Catholic Reformation, show how it responded to Protestant criticism, and how it created the modern Catholic Church.

Glossary of Names and Terms

1. Thomas à Kempis: author of *The Imitation of Christ*, an example of the Catholic movement toward pietism and mysticism just before the Reformation.

2. Wittenberg: German city where Martin Luther posted his *Ninety-five Theses*, which precipitated the Protestant Reformation.

3. Edict of Worms: imperial decree branding Luther a criminal and ordering that his books be burned as heresy.

4. Katherina von Bora: former nun whom Luther married, providing a model for the Protestant ministry of the future.

5. Thomas More: former Lord Chancellor of England who supported the pope's refusal to grant Henry VIII a divorce and was beheaded as a traitor.

6. Calvinism: the form of Protestantism originated and led by John Calvin, centered at Geneva, which spread more widely than any other branch of the movement.

7. Society of Jesus: founded by Ignatius of Loyola, this religious order became the most powerful instrument of the Catholic Reformation.

8. Council of Trent: meeting of Catholic leaders from 1545 to 1563 which dealt with abuses and created the modern Church.

9. Edict of Nantes: decree from King Henry IV that established Catholicism as the official religion of France but gave freedom of worship to Huguenots.

10. Act of Uniformity: made the Book of Common Prayer standard for worship in England and essentially established the Protestant Church of England.

Match the Following Words with their Definitions

1. Johann Eck

2. Philip Melanchthon

3. Katherina von Bora

4. Ulrich Zwingli

5. Munster

6. Menno Simons

7. Thomas Cranmer

8. Anne Boleyn

9. Francis Xavier

10. Henry IV

A. Nun who married Martin Luther

B. Henry VIII's second wife

C. Pacifist leader of Dutch Anabaptists

D. City declared by radical Anabaptists to be the New Jerusalem

E. Huguenot who became a Catholic to gain a crown

F. Luther's opponent in the Leipzig debate

G. Jesuit missionary to India and Japan

H. Archbishop of Canterbury who granted Henry VIII's divorce

I. Lutheran scholar who became known as "Teacher of Germany"

J. Leader of the Swiss Reformed Church movement

Choose the Correct Answer

1. The Christian humanists were

    a. Pessimistic about the future of humanity
    b. Realistic about their dreams for the church
    c. Supported by wealthy German patrons
    d. Doubtful about the benefits of education
    e. Frequently on the run from the law

2. Erasmus hoped to reform Christianity through all of the following *except*

    a. Spreading the radical reform ideas of Luther
    b. Ridiculing the abuses of the church
    c. Providing readers a New Testament in the original Greek
    d. Teaching the "philosophy of Christ" as a guide for daily life
    e. Showing people how to return to the simplicity of the early church

3. In his book *Utopia* Thomas More

    a. Argued that Christians could not be humanists
    b. Heralded the coming of Martin Luther
    c. Outlined a harmonious social order with communal property
    d. Argued that Henry VIII was wrong to want a divorce
    e. Defended the rights of the Huguenots

4. Popular religion in the late Middle Ages and Renaissance witnessed a

    a. Revival of mysticism called the Modern Devotion
    b. Decline in interest in sacred relics
    c. Decline in the sale of indulgences for remission of sins
    d. Careful and comprehensive reform of church practices
    e. Demanded that kings revive the Crusades

5. Martin Luther's early monastic life was characterized by

    a. A tendency to forget his daily ritual duties
    b. An obsession with his own sinfulness
    c. His devotion to the study of canon law
    d. Rejection of the Bible as the Word of God
    e. Occasional dalliance with local women

6. Luther finally answered the question "How can I be saved?" by

    a. The doctrine of justification by grace through faith
    b. Doing good works aimed at achieving universal brotherhood
    c. Following the Rule of the Augustinian Order
    d. Taking the sacraments every day
    e. Leaving monastic life to marry and have children

7. Luther and Zwingli parted company over the issue of the

   a. Separation of church and state
   b. Ordination and priesthood of women
   c. Use of musical instruments in the church
   d. Doctrine of the Lord's Supper
   e. Whether ministers should marry

8. The Edict of Worms

   a. Included Luther's statement "Here I stand"
   b. Expressed Luther's feelings about the authority of Leo X
   c. Called on Luther to appear before Charles V to recant his heresies
   d. Protected Luther so long as he remained in Saxony
   e. Made Luther an outlaw within the Holy Roman Empire

9. The Peasants' War of 1524-1525 was

   a. Inspired by the writings of Lutheran theologian Philip Melanchthon
   b. One reason Lutheranism spread so quickly throughout Europe
   c. Applauded by Luther for helping bring down Catholicism
   d. A revolt by people of rising expectations against their local lords
   e. Instrumental in making Henry IV King of France

10. The Swiss leader Zwingli

   a. Instituted his reforms after a military coup in Zurich
   b. Favored elaborate church ceremonies on Christmas and Easter
   c. Stressed the need for state supervision over the church
   d. Preserved remnants of papal Christianity such as confession
   e. Was condemned to death by the Calvinist Consistory

11. The immediate cause of the English Reformation was

   a. Continual papal interference in affairs of state
   b. The influence of Luther's life and writings in England
   c. Cardinal Wolsey's plot against Henry VIII
   d. Queen Catherine's failure to produce a male heir
   e. Thomas More's weak defense of papal authority

12. Find the *false* description among the following officials of Henry VIII

   a. Thomas More---Lord Chancellor executed for not accepting King Henry's authority over the church
   b. Thomas Cranmer---Archbishop of Canterbury executed for refusing to annul the king's marriage
   c. Thomas Cromwell---principal secretary who confiscated monasteries to bolster the treasury without royal authority
   d. Cardinal Wolsey---Lord Chancellor who tried but failed to gain a papal annulment of the king's marriage
   e. Clement VII---Medici pope who found it politically impossible to grant Henry's petition for divorce

13. The reign of England's Queen Mary I was noted for

    a. Her failure to restore Catholicism
    b. Constant warfare with her Spanish territories
    c. An end to the English Reformation
    d. Her Act of Supremacy in 1534
    e. The heir she produced after she was 40

14. Which of the following statements best describes the reform movement of John Calvin?

    a. Its rejection of Luther's doctrine of "justification by faith alone" gave it a Catholic tone
    b. Its doctrine of Predestination made it essentially a passive faith
    c. Its belief that men must "obey God rather than man" made Calvinists willing to rebel against secular power
    d. Its conviction that God watches man's deeds kept it from interfering in people's private lives
    e. Its mysticism made it grant individual members the right to interpret the Bible as their "inner light" directed them

15. Calvin's doctrine of Predestination

    a. Taught that material wealth was a sign of being one of the elect
    b. Made Calvinists more certain than other Christians that they were doing God's will on earth
    c. Assumed that God had predestined the male to be the head of the family and society
    d. Was within his lifetime added to most Protestant confessions of faith
    e. Never caught on with his followers and was abandoned after his death

16. Typically in Protestant societies

    a. Women were encouraged to pursue public careers
    b. Women were restricted to the roles of wife and mother
    c. The celibate life was considered superior to marriage
    d. Children were never physically punished
    e. No child remained at home after age 18

17. Protestant educators

    a. Retained humanist principles of pedagogy and curriculum
    b. Attempted to educate as large a percentage of the population as possible
    c. Sought to produce both good pastors and good state servants
    d. Divided students into classes based on age and capabilities
    e. Did all of the above

18. At the Council of Trent, the Catholic Church

    a. Established a clear body of doctrine under a supreme pontiff
    b. Upheld the right, under certain circumstances, of the church to sell indulgences
    c. Reaffirmed the doctrine of Purgatory but made no statement about Transubstantiation
    d. Established the authority for doctrine on tradition above scripture
    e. Made clerical celibacy a personal choice

19. In France just prior to the Wars of Religion there

    a. The nobility was between 40and 50 percent Huguenot
    b. The general population was evenly split between Huguenots and Catholics
    c. Catherine de Medici's succeeded in suppressing most Protestant dissent
    d. A wealthy Catholic majority lorded over a poverty stricken Huguenot minority
    e. John Calvin made a triumphal tour, converting many Catholics

20. The French Wars of Religion (1562-1598)

    a. Ended when the Huguenots won a decisive battle in the field
    b. Ended when Henry IV guaranteed rights both to Catholics and Huguenots
    c. Ended on Saint Bartholomew's Day with a Huguenot massacre
    d. Were entire a French affair, without ties to conflicts elsewhere
    e. Ended only when Louis XIV banished all Protestants from France

Complete the Following Sentences

1. Thomas More's ideal society, outlined in his book _____, was not at all like the real world where he died because he would not approve the _____ of King _____.

2. Martin Luther, an _____ monk, criticized the sales of _____ in his famous _____ Theses.

3. In the greatest social upheaval of his lifetime, the Peasants War, Luther sided with the German _____ against the German _____. Order was necessary, he argued, for the spread of the _____.

4. Ulrich Zwingli ultimately failed in his attempt to unite the reformed churches of _____ and _____ when he and Luther could not agree on the meaning of the _____.

5. The Anabaptist movement got a bad image when a radical group called _____ set up their "Kingdom of God" at the German city of _____, calling it the _____ _____.

6. Thomas Cranmer helped Henry VIII divorce Queen _____ and marry _____, then moved England toward Protestantism under Henry's heir, _____.

7. John Calvin's emphasis in his great book, _____ ____ _____ _____ _____, was on the absolute _____ of God, which led him to defend the doctrine of _____.

8. Protestantism took away women's religious profession, the life of a nun, and said they must be only _____ and _____, a "gladsome" punishment for the sin of _____.

9. Henry of Navarre left the _____ faith to become a _____ in order to gain the throne of _____.

10. When convinced that _____ planned to depose her in favor of her cousin _____, Queen Elizabeth of England had her rival _____.

Place the Following in Chronological Order and Give Dates

1. Society of Jesus recognized   1.

2. English Act of Supremacy   2.

3. Council of Trent convenes   3.

4. Diet of Worms   4.

5. Destruction of the Spanish Armada   5.

6. John Calvin publishes his *Institutes* 6.

7. Schmalkaldic League formed   7.

Questions for Critical Thought

1. Describe northern Renaissance humanism, and show how it differed from that of its earlier form in Italy.

2. What conditions in the Church of the early sixteenth century made the Reformation both possible and probable? What part did Erasmus play in pointing them out?

3. Describe Martin Luther's part in the Protestant revolt. What personal qualities made Luther act as he did, and how did his actions affect the course of the Reformation?

4. Explain how the Anabaptists differed from the Lutherans. Why did even Protestants such as Luther despise and fear them?

5. Discuss the Reformation in England. What caused it? How did it differ from the Reformation in other places? What were its results?

6. Describe the work of John Calvin and the development of Calvinism? Explain why and how he came to have such widespread influence in Protestantism?

7. What shape did the Catholic Reformation take? How did the reformed Catholic Church differ from Protestantism? How well did its reforms prepare it for future ages?

8. Why were the various wars of religion across the continent of Europe so bloody? Why did the participants emphasize their differences and fight so hard to suppress opposition?

Analysis of Primary Source Documents

1. What did Erasmus find ridiculous about monastic practices of his day? Describe his method of poking fun at what he considered absurdities.

2. Why did Martin Luther's classroom exercise, The Ninety-Five Theses, cause such a sensation and have such an impact on his society and times?

3. Compare and contrast the Luther who was a rebel against ecclesiastical authority with the Luther who wrote the treatise against the peasants. How do you account for the differences?

4. Using his comments at the Marburg Colloquy as your guide, draw as many conclusions as you can about Luther's personality, mind, and public manner.

5. Give examples of how John Calvin's Genevan Consistory controlled the personal lives of citizens. What kind of city did its discipline create?

6. If Catherine Zell is a typical Anabaptist, what new themes did this movement bring to Christianity? To what extent were these themes the natural consequences of Luther's doctrinal innovations?

7. If one follows Loyola's formula for correct Christian thinking, what does the true Christian believe? How does the true Christian act? What does the true Christian accomplish?

8. How does Queen Elizabeth's speech before Parliament in 1601 demonstrate her political acumen? To what extent did being an unmarried woman add to the image she adopted as her public *persona*?

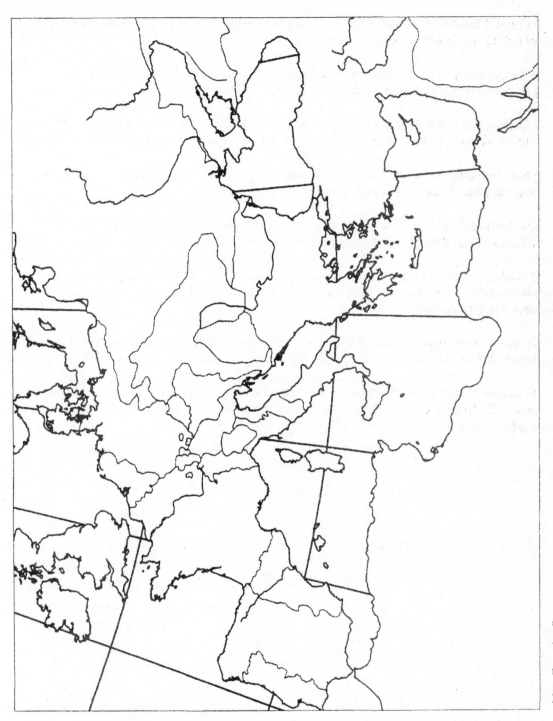

Map Exercise 8

Map Exercise 8: The Empire of Charles V

Shade and label the possessions of Charles V and with various other shades show the territories of other princes in his time

1. Aragon
2. Austria
3. Bavaria
4. Bohemia
5. Brandenburg
6. Castile
7. France
8. Holy Roman Empire
9. Hungary
10. Netherlands
11. Ottoman Empire
12. Papal States
13. Poland
14. Portugal
15. Russia
16. Saxony
17. Switzerland
18. Tuscany

CHAPTER 14
EUROPE AND THE WORLD:
NEW ENCOUNTERS, 1500-1800

Chapter Outline

I. On the Brink of a New World
    A. Motives for European Exploration
        1. Fascination with the East
        2. Wealth through Trade
        3. Christian Missions
    B. Technological Means Needed

II. New Horizons: The Portuguese and Spanish Empires
    A. Portuguese Maritime Empire
        1. Prince Henry, the Navigator
        2. Bartholomew Dias around the Cape
        3. Vasco da Gama to India
        4. China
    B. Voyages to the New World
        1. Christopher Columbus
        2. John Cabot
        3. Balboa and Magellan
        4. Treaty of Tordesillas
    C. Spanish Empire in the New World
        1. Early Civilizations in Mesoamerica
        2. Spanish Conquest of the Aztec Empire
        3. Hernan Cortes and Mexico
        4. Francisco Pizarro and Peru
        5. Administration of the Spanish Empire
        6. Bartolomé de Las Casas

III. New Rivals on the World Stage: Dutch, British, and French
    A. Africa: The Slave Trade
        1. Growth of the Slave Trade
        2. Effects and End of Slave Trade
    B. The West in Southeast Asia
    C. The French and British in India
    D. China: Ming and Qing Dynasties
    E. Japan
    F. The Americas
        1. British North America
        2. French North America

IV. Impact of European Expansion
    A. The Conquered
       1. Catholic Missionaries
    B. The Conquerors

V. Toward a World Economy
    A. Economic Conditions in the Sixteenth Century
    B. Growth of Commercial Capitalism
    C. Mercantilism
    D. Overseas Trade and Colonies: A Global Economy

Chapter Summary

    The energies unleashed by the Renaissance and the rivalries unleashed by the Reformation made the sixteenth and seventeenth centuries an era of discovery, expansion, and commerce. It was an age of danger, opportunity, and achievement.

    Long fascinated by the world beyond their shores, Europeans in the late fifteenth century had the technological skills finally to go exploring; and what they found expanded both their minds and their treasuries. First the Portuguese and Spanish, then the Dutch, English, and French sent out expeditions that resulted in empires in the "New World" discovered by Columbus and in the older world of Asia. Between 1500 and 1800 European came to dominate, both culturally and economically, much of the known world.

    With ships linking far flung empires, the world of commercial capitalism was born. Nations attempted to enrich themselves through centrally controlled systems of mercantilism; but their efforts proved only partially successful. Mercantilism was doomed ultimately to failure as the first global economy, with multiple interdependencies evolved.

    The discoveries, conquests, and organization of empires did not come freely. Native peoples were subjugated and enslaved; natural resources were depleted; and the conquerors each year were more convinced of the superiority of their culture and race. The twenty-first century is surrounded by the structures and rubble of Europe's first encounter with the rest of the world.

Learning Objectives

1.   Be able to explain the motives that fueled Europe's early modern overseas exploration and expansion and the new technologies that made it possible.

2.   Be able to describe the way the Portuguese were able to establish an overseas empire and the way it functioned.

3.   Be able to describe the creation and characteristics of the Spanish Empire in the Americas.

4.   Be able to discuss the economic philosophies that dominated Europe and the way they affected the world economy Europeans established.

5.   Be able to explain the religious, social, and economic effects of European conquests around the globe on both the conquerors and those they conquered.

Glossary of Names and Terms

1. John Mandeville: author of a book of fantasy literature about the wonders of the world beyond Europe, the inspiration for many foreign voyages.

2. Henry the Navigator: member of the Portuguese royal family who founded a school for navigators and encouraged exploration down the west coast of Africa.

3. Columbus: attempted to reach Asia by sailing west into the Atlantic and in the process landed in a "new world."

4. Tordesillas: a city on the border of Spain and Portugal where a treaty dividing the pagan world between the two countries was blessed by the pope.

5. *Encomienda*: Spanish royal system which allowed conquerors to use Indians as labor but required that they convert them to Christianity and protect them from abuse.

6. Bartolemé de las Casas: Dominican friar whose writings exposed the cruelty of the Spanish against the Indians and led to reforms in the imperial system.

7. Dutch East India Company: financial organization that made huge profits in the Indonesian archipelago and set the stage for the creation of the Dutch Empire there.

8. Robert Clive: British military commander who established his country's supremacy over both native rulers and other Europeans powers in India.

9. Samuel de Champlain: founder of the first French settlement in North America, at Quebec, which set the stage for the establishment of New France.

10. Mercantilism: the dominant economic theory of early modern Europe, which assumed that the total volume of trade was unchangeable and that each country must gain and keep as large a percentage of it as possible.

Match the Following Words with their Definitions

1. Prester John

2. Albuquerque

3. Ferdinand Magellan

4. Treaty of Tordesillas

5. Francesco Pizarro

6. Plassey

7. Champlain

8. Mestizo

9. Mulatto

10. Gerardus Mercator

A. Person of mixed European and African bloodlines

B. Mythical figure that inspired Portuguese exploration to the east

C. Agreement which divided non-Christian lands between Spain and Portugal

D. Person of mixed European and Indian bloodlines

E. Spanish explorer whose expedition was the first to circumnavigate the earth

F. Established the first French settlement in Canada

G. Naval cartographer

H. Sit of British victory over Mughals

I. Spanish general who conquered the Incan Empire

J. Established Portuguese trading post of Goa

Choose the Correct Answer

1. Portuguese expansionism was inspired by

   a. Missionary zeal to convert the lost peoples of the Americas
   b. A desire to catch up with the Spanish
   c. Severe droughts that had left Portugal without an adequate food supply
   d. Strong support from members of the royal family
   e. The preaching, throughout Portugal, of Prester John

2. Spanish exploration of and expansion into the New World is best exemplified by

   a. Amerigo Vespucci's circumnavigation of the globe
   b. Hernan Cortes' conquest of the Aztec Empire
   c. Ferdinand Magellan's conquest of the Incas
   d. Vasco da Gama's successes in Calicut
   e. Francisco Pizarro's discovery of the Pacific Ocean

3. The name America that was given to the New World came from Amerigo Vespucci:

   a. A Spanish pirate
   b. An Italian writer
   c. An Italian missionary
   d. A Portuguese governmental official
   e. The first governor of New Spain

4. The Treaty of Tordesillas

   a. Was forced on Spain by the pope
   b. Showed the rising international power of France
   c. Divided the non-European world between Portugal and Spain
   d. Ended the Thirty Years' War
   e. Had its greatest impact on North America

5.   Hernan Cortes was aided in his conquest of the Aztecs by

    a.   Moctezuma's loss of self-confidence
    b.   Other tribes hostile to the Aztecs
    c.   An outbreak of smallpox
    d.   Spanish certainty that they represented God
    e.   All of the above

6.   The *encomienda* system

    a.   Exploited native Americans to enrich Spaniards
    b.   Protected native Americans against capitalists
    c.   Gave the Jesuits administrative control over the West Indies
    d.   Failed to be approved in the Spanish cortes
    e.   Was defended by de las Casas

7.   Bartholomé de las Casas, a Dominican monk, was known for his

    a.   Cruel and barbarous treatment of Indians
    b.   Magnificent lifestyle on a Cuban plantation
    c.   Revelations about the cruel treatment of Indians under Spanish rule
    d.   Creation of the Native American Catholic church
    e.   Translation of Native American poetry into English

8.   The Boers were

    a.   German mercenaries who helped the Dutch establish colonies in India
    b.   Dutch farmers who settled in South Africa
    c.   An Order of Franciscan missionaries to China
    d.   Dutch businessmen who developed silver mines in South Africa
    e.   A destructive insect that destroyed many South American crops

9.   Trade in African slaves increased in the early sixteenth century because

    a.   Wealthy Europeans came to view them as symbols of wealth
    b.   Victorious African tribes sought new markets for their conquered enemies
    c.   Sugar production in the West Indies demanded ever more laborers
    d.   Africans were well suited by nature to work in the tropics
    e.   No one spoke out against the slave trade

10. One effect of the slave trade on the African nation of Benin was an increase in

    a.   The overall health of the population left behind
    b.   Religious devotion to traditional gods
    c.   Violent attacks on European diplomats
    d.   The practice of human sacrifice
    e.   The rise of a wealthy black middle class

11. During the seventeenth century the Dutch replaced the Portuguese and English as

   a. Chief merchants of the Asian spice trade
   b. The most successful missionaries to Africa
   c. Colonial masters of southeast Asia
   d. Managers of the sugar plantations of the West Indies
   e. The most powerful Protestant force in the world

12. The effects of the Seven Years' War on India was

   a. An increase of Portuguese influence
   b. The complete withdrawal of France
   c. Independence for the city-state of Calcutta
   d. The establishment of the Anglican Church
   e. Severe famine and a decline in population

13. In 1644 China was changed by a victory of the

   a. Manchus over the Ming dynasty
   b. British over the French
   c. Ming dynasty over Qing raiders
   d. Great Kahn over British troops
   e. Christian missionaries over Muslim rulers

14. The Tokugawa rulers of Japan

   a. Were Japan's first Christian dynasty
   b. Created the term shogun to describe benevolent rule
   c. Established the most powerful shogunate in Japanese history
   d. Built one of the world's largest navies
   e. Lasted only a few years, until the British mandate

15. France lost its North American empire due in part to its inability to

   a. Develop institutions that suited the harsh climate
   b. Produce capable military commanders
   c. Stave off Indian attacks
   d. Get more French settlers to emigrate to the New World
   e. Fight battles in cold weather

16. Juana Inés de la Cruz advocated the

   a. Erection of forts along the Saint Lawrence River
   b. Establishment of publishing houses to print Bibles in Native American languages
   c. Education of Native American women
   d. Equality of men and women in the New World
   e. Elevation of Mother Anna Matera to sainthood

17. The Jesuits in Japan annulled their early missionary successes by

   a. Encouraging rebellion against the imperial family
   b. Destroying native religious shrines
   c. Engaging in questionable business affairs
   d. Discouraging young men from becoming shogun soldiers
   e. Requiring converts to give up all but one of their wives

18. The Mercator projection aided sea captains because it

   a. Gave them a perfect picture of the earth's surface
   b. Allowed them to sail at night and in bad weather
   c. Cut through ice
   d. Provided them with true lines of direction
   e. Was available in all European languages

19. The tie between European banking and the mining industry is best illustrated by

   a. Philip II's grant of gold mining rights in Peru to the Pizarro family
   b. Charles I's grant of mining monopolies to Jacob Fugger
   c. William of Orange's grant of monopolies in the Hudson Valley to the Bourse
   d. James I's grant of monopolies to the London Company
   e. Louis XIV's grant of monopolies in Quebec to Jacques Cartier

20. Under the mercantile system, nations sought to increase their share of the

   a. World's gold and silver bullion holdings
   b. Number of slaves traded annually worldwide
   c. Small businesses within their countries
   d. Missionary responsibility for converting the pagans
   e. Logging and fur enterprises in North America

Complete the Following Sentences

1. Encouraged by the support of Prince Henry, known as the _____ , Portuguese sailor _____ ___ _____ found a sea route to India, where Alfonso __ _____ established an outpost that started an empire of trade.

2. In the Americas, Spaniard _____ _____ conquered the Aztecs, while _____ _____ conquered the Incas. Spanish treatment of Native Americans was later publicized by the monk Bartolome ___ _____ _____ .

3. The *encomienda* system permitted the Spanish to use Native Americans as _____ but also required them to _____ them and see to their _____ needs.

4. African slaves were packed into cargo ships _____ to· _____ per ship for voyages that took as least _____ day, during which time an average of _____ % of them died.

5.   Sir Robert Clive began the British consolidation of power in _____ when his army of _____ defeated a much larger Mughal-led army at _____.

6.   In 1793 Britain's Lord _____ pressed the Chinese government to open cities other than _____ for foreign trade; but he was rebuffed by Emperor _____.

7.   Japanese fears of foreign influence led first to their expulsion of _____ and then to the regulation that Dutch traders could visit only the port of _____ for no more than _____ months per year.

8.   The thirteen British North American colonies had their own _____; and their merchants _____ and _____ all British attempts at colonial regulation.

9.   The mercantile system assumed that the volume of trade was _____ and that economic activity was a form of _____ to determine which nations would prosper at the _____ of others.

10.   The way European expansion affected the ecology of conquered lands is demonstrated by the introduction of beef _____ into the Americas, _____ _____ into the West Indies, and American _____ into Africa.

Place the Following in Chronological Order and Give Dates

1.   First African slaves arrive in America   1.

2.   Battle of Plassey   2.

3.   French cede Canada to Britain   3.

4.   Treaty of Tordesillas   4.

5.   Champlain establishes settlement in Quebec   5.

6.   Dutch seize Malacca   6.

7.   Dias rounds the point of Africa   7.

Questions for Critical Thought

1.   Discuss the factors that encouraged and enabled Europeans to enter their period of expansion around the globe in the sixteenth century.

2.   Describe the empire which the Spanish established in the Americas: its government, its social and religious systems, its economy, its strengths and weaknesses.

3.   Describe and explain the rise of the African slave trade: its causes, objectives, and results for American history.

4. Discuss the first European attempts to create spheres of influence in Asia. Why did they succeed in some places and fail in others?

5. Compare the British and French colonies in North America. What accounts for the British success and the French failure?

6. Explain the effects European colonization of the Americas and some of Asia had on the conquered people and their conquerors.

7. Describe the development of commercial capitalism in the seventeenth and eighteenth centuries. How did Europe become the world's most prosperous region?

8. Was the economy of the eighteenth century truly "global" in the contemporary sense? Explain why you think it was or was not.

Analysis of Primary Source Documents

1. How does Albuquerque's rationale for the conquest of Malacca demonstrate his loyalty to his two lords, God and the king? How was he able to make the two loyalties agree?

2. What did Columbus see as his two purposes in making the land he discovered a part of the Spanish Empire? Why did he believe this would easily be accomplished?

3. What did Cortés think of the Aztec civilization he conquered? What does he indicate made him feel justified in destroying it? What does this say about his own Spanish civilization?

4. Try to separate fact from fiction in de las Casas' account of the treatment of Native Americans by Spanish conquistadors. Is there enough fact and is it serious enough to cause a conscientious Spanish official to order changes? If so, how would you suggest he start?

5. What characteristics of the African slave trade did the Frenchman you have read find odious? How would a slave trader likely have justified his occupation against such criticism?

6. What assumptions lie behind Louis XIV's letter to the King of Tonkin? How was the Asian king able to respond to Louis with dignity but without giving offense?

7. How did the Chinese emperor's reply to Lord Macartney differ from Tonkin's reply to Louis? What does this reply say about Chinese attitudes toward foreigners?

8. What kind of social and economic system did the Jesuits establish in southern South America? What did Felix de Azara find objectionable about it all?

Map Exercise 9: European Overseas Possessions in 1658

Shade and label the following

1. Angola
2. Brazil
3. Caribbean Sea
4. India
5. Indian Ocean
6. Indonesia
7. Mozambique
8. New Spain
9. Peru
10. Philippines
11. Portugal
12. Spain

Pinpoint and label the following

1. Calicut
2. Canton
3. Ceylon
4. Colombo
5. Goa
6. Lima
7. Macao
8. Tenochtitlan
9. Zanzibar

CHAPTER 15
STATE BUILDING AND THE SEARCH
FOR ORDER
IN THE SEVENTEENTH CENTURY

Chapter Outline

I.   Social Crises, War, and Rebellion
     A.   Witchcraft Craze
          1.   The Spread of Witchcraft
          2.   Decline
     B.   Thirty Years' War (1618-1648)
          1.   Background to the War
          2.   The Bohemian Phase
          3.   Danish Phase
          4.   Swedish Phase
          5.   Franco-Swedish Phase
     C.   A Military Revolution?
     D.   Rebellions

II. Practice of Absolutism: Western Europe
     A.   Absolute Monarchy in France
          1.   Cardinal Richelieu's Centralization of Power under Louis XIII
          2.   Cardinal Mazarin during the Minority of Louis XIV
     B.   Reign of Louis XIV (1643-1715)
          1.   Administration of the Government
          2.   Religious Policy
          3.   Financial Issues
          4.   Daily Life at the Court of Versailles
          5.   The Wars of Louis XIV
     C.   Decline of Spain
          1.   The Reign of Philip IV

III. Absolutism in Central, Eastern, and Northern Europe
     A.   German States
          1.   Brandenburg-Prussia
               a.   House of Hohenzollern
               b.   Frederick William's Army and his Commissariat
               c.   Elector Frederick III Becomes King Frederick I
          2.   Emergence of Austria
               a.   House of Habsburg
               b.   Leopold I's Move to the East
               c.   Multicultural Empire

B. Italy: From Spanish to Austrian Rule
    C. Russia: from Fledgling Principality to Major Power
        1. Reign of Ivan IV, the Terrible
        2. Reign of Peter I, (the Great) Romanov (1689-1725)
            a. Centralization of Authority
            b. Westernization
            c. Peter's Wars
    D. Great Northern States: Denmark and Sweden
    E. Ottoman Empire: Suleiman I
    F. Limits of Absolutism

IV. Limited Monarchy and Republics
    A. Weakness of the Polish Monarchy
        1. Elective System
        2. Confederation of Estates
    B. Golden Age of the Dutch Republic
        1. Independence following the Peace of Westphalia
        2. Economic Prosperity
        3. Amsterdam as a Commercial Capital
    C. England and the Emergence of Constitutional Monarchy
        1. James I and Parliament
        2. Charles I and Civil War
        3. Oliver Cromwell and the Commonwealth
        4. The Stuart Restoration and Charles II
        5. James II and a "Glorious Revolution"
        6. William and Mary and the Bill of Rights
        7. Responses to the English Revolution
            a. Thomas Hobbes and *Leviathan*
            b. John Locke and the Right of Revolution

V. The Flourishing of European Culture
    A. The Changing Faces of Art
        1. Mannerism: El Greco
        2. Baroque: Bernini and Gentileschi
        3. French Classicism: Poussin
        4. Dutch Realism: Leyster and Rembrandt
    B. Wondrous Age of Theater
        1. Shakespeare
        2. Lope de Vega
        3. Racine
        4. Molière

Chapter Summary

The political and religious crises of the sixteenth and early seventeenth centuries, with terrors, wars, and rebellions, led philosophers and rulers to consider alternatives to what they considered the insecure and often chaotic institutional structures of the day. For over a century both groups defended the growth of strong monarchies that could keep the peace and order, who could enforce social uniformity, who could take measures to increase national prosperity.

Government moved increasingly toward absolutism, toward kings stronger than any known in Europe before, kings with power to provide order and prosperity. While absolutism reached its apex in France with the reign of Louis XIV, it had significant successes in Spain, the German states, Italy, Russia, and the Ottoman Empire. Everywhere there was a movement toward centralized power, the weakening of local rulers, and state control of economies.

Only in a few nations did royal power diminish and begin to share rule with parliamentary and constitutional systems. It did happen in Poland, in the United Provinces of Holland, and most importantly in Britain. In the latter there occurred in 1688 a bloodless revolution against James II, whom Parliament replaced with the dual monarchy of William and Mary, who promised certain rights to British citizens. There the way was paved not only for limited monarchy but also for democracy.

This Age of Absolutism was an age of cultural and philosophical achievement. El Greco's Mannerism and Bernini's Baroque styles were succeeded by the French Classicism of Poussin and the Dutch Realism of Rembrandt. It was an age when the French theater caught up with Shakespeare's English style and gained world dominance, as demonstrated by the work of Molière and Racine. It was a time of ferment in political theory: the penetrating analyses of Thomas Hobbes and John Locke. The Enlightenment was beginning.

Learning Objectives

1. Be able to analyze the causes and consequences of the witchcraft craze of seventeenth century Europe.

2. Be able to describe the absolute monarchy of France, how it was established, how it functioned, and its effects on the nation.

3. Be able to trace the rise of Russia to its status as a world power, giving particular attention to the life and work of Peter Romanov.

4. Be able to follow the progression of the English monarchy during the seventeenth century and to show both how it survived its rocky road and why it did not end.

5. Be able to account for the dramatic flowering of European culture during the seventeenth century, particularly in art and literature, and discuss the achievements of its finest figures.

Glossary of Names and Terms

1. Peace of Westphalia: ended the Thirty Years' War by separating politics from religion and making the settlement along purely political lines.

2. Jacques Bossuet: advocate of the divine right of kings, by which their power was absolute and could not be disobeyed.

3. Cardinal Richelieu: chief minister to Louis XIII who established the administration under which the French kings could become absolute.

4. Edict of Fontainebleau: Louis XIV's attempt to make France Catholic by destroying Huguenot churches and schools, causing a mass emigration of skilled artisans.

5. Versailles: Louis XIV's grand palace, where he established his court and which he used to centralize the French government.

6. Gaspar de Guzman: his attempts to increase the power of the Spanish monarchy failed due to the number and strength of the aristocracy.

7. St. Petersburg: Peter Romanov's new capital city, built in the far north of Russia to rival the splendors of Versailles.

8. Glorious Revolution: the Protestant victory that exiled England's Catholic James I and brought William and Mary of Orange to the throne.

9. *Leviathan:* political work by Thomas Hobbes which defended absolute rule as the only way to provide a secure and proper life for citizens.

10. Rembrandt: greatest painter of the Dutch Golden Age who rejected material success to follow his own vision and died bankrupt.

Match the Following Words with their Definitions

1. Mazarin

2. Fronde

3. Versailles

4. Oliver Cromwell

5. Bill of Rights

6. Thomas Hobbes

7. John Locke

8. El Greco

9. Nicholas Poussin

10. Jean-Baptist Racine

A. Argued that if a monarch broke his social contract, the people had the right to form a new government

B. Granted Parliament the right to levy taxes

C. Leader of the British Commonwealth

D. Mannerist master

E. Argued that order demanded absolute monarchy

F.   Made use of themes taken from Greek tragedy

G.   Center of Louis XIV's royal government

H.   Rebellion of the French nobility against the royal family

I.   Exemplified the principles of French Classicism

J.   Directed the French government when Louis XIV was a child

Choose the Correct Answer

1.   One result of seventeenth century crises in Europe was

     a.   An increased role of the church in secular society
     b.   A trend toward democratic reforms in government
     c.   The division of empires into smaller feudal kingdoms
     d.   A trend toward absolutism, as exemplified by Louis XIV
     e.   The rise in the number of slaves working there

2.   As Louis XIII's chief minister, Cardinal Richelieu was most successful in

     a.   Evicting the Huguenots from France
     b.   Strengthening the central role of the monarchy
     c.   Creating a reservoir of funds for the treasury
     d.   Emerging victorious in the Fronde revolts
     e.   Recruiting missionaries to go to China

3.   The series of noble revolts known as the Fronde resulted in

     a.   The assassination in 1661 of Cardinal Mazarin
     b.   Increased power for the Parlement of Paris
     c.   A stronger, more secure, more unified royal army
     d.   Many Frenchmen looking to the crown for stability
     e.   The early coronation of Louis XIII's heir

4.   Louis XIV was most successful in controlling the administration of his kingdom by

     a.   Working closely with hereditary, aristocratic officeholders
     b.   Using his intendants as direct royal agents
     c.   Employing royal patronage to "bribe" officers to execute the king's policies
     d.   Eliminating town councils and legislative bodies in the provinces
     e.   Putting military officers in charge of judicial hearings

5.   Louis XIV restructured the policy-making machinery of the French government by

     a.   Personally dominating the actions of his ministers and secretaries
     b.   Stacking the royal council with high nobles and royal princes
     c.   Selecting his ministers from established aristocratic families
     d.   Personally hearing every judicial case that was appealed from lower courts
     e.   Advancing personally through every office, learning all their skills

6. Louis XIV's military adventures resulted in

    a. French domination of Western Europe
    b. Defeat after defeat by coalitions of nations
    c. The union of the thrones of France and Spain
    d. Increased popular support for Louis in France
    e. The final victory of the French over the British worldwide

7. Activities at the court of Versailles included all of the following *except*

    a. Evenings of concerts, games, and banquets
    b. Attempts by aristocrats to catch the ear of the monarch
    c. Invitations to challenge Louis' authority
    d. A system of etiquette that depended on the whim of the monarch
    e. Activities designed to demean noble visitors

8. The overall practical purpose of the Palace of Versailles was to

    a. Control and limit the power of the aristocracy
    b. Keep Louis' queen and mistresses happy
    c. Act as a reception hall for foreign visitors
    d. Give Louis a life of absolute privacy
    e. Allow Louis to recover from respiratory problems

9. During the seventeenth century Spain

    a. Grew rich off the spoils of its American colonies
    b. Lost most of her European possessions outside Iberia
    c. Curtailed the power of the Catholic Church
    d. Saw the emergence of a dominant middle class
    e. Benefited from the work of competent kings and first ministers

10. The Russian "Time of Troubles" describes a

    a. Period of anarchy before the rise of the Romanov dynasty
    b. Time of religious turmoil in which many Old Believers committed suicide
    c. Period of revolt led by Cossack Stenka Razin
    d. Part of the reign of Alexander I, when he reestablished serfdom in Russia
    e. Time of continual foreign invasion and famine

11. The cultural reforms of Peter the Great

    a. Failed to change habits of dress and grooming
    b. Left the Orthodox Church untouched
    c. Required Russian men to wear beards
    d. Permitted Russian women many new freedoms
    e. Required the use of French in all public schools

12. In his efforts to Europeanize Russia, Peter

    a. Required that Orthodox priests marry
    b. Reorganized the government so that the Duma shared power with him
    c. Adopted mercantilist policies to stimulate growth of the economy
    d. Built a "police state" with the aid of aristocratic bureaucrats
    e. Lowered taxes to stimulate free enterprise among the peasants

13. Peter's primary foreign policy goal was to

    a. Open a Russian warm-water port accessible to Europe
    b. Bring an end to the Ottoman Empire
    c. Defeat and control the Scandinavian countries
    d. Make Germany a Russian dependency
    e. Win a seat on the European Council of Elders

14. The most successful absolute rulers of the seventeenth century were those who

    a. Used traditional systems of administration to their advantage
    b. Completely crushed the power of the landed aristocracy
    c. Dominated the lives of their subjects at every level
    d. Established strict rules of dress and public behavior
    e. Held public executions as examples of the results of rebellion

15. Between 1688 and 1832, Britain's government was in fact, if not in name

    a. A plutocracy---ruled by the rich
    b. An oligarchy---ruled by an elite
    c. A theocracy---ruled by religious leaders
    d. An absolute monarchy---ruled by an all-powerful sovereign
    e. A democracy---ruled by the people

16. The British Declaration of Rights and Bill of Rights

    a. Laid the foundation for a constitutional monarchy
    b. Resolved England's seventeenth-century religious feuds
    c. Reaffirmed the divine-right theory of kingship
    d. Gave the king the right to raise armies without consent of Parliament
    e. Ended the monarchy for the eleven years of the Protectorate

17. The "Leviathan" of which Thomas Hobbes wrote was a

    a. Snake that killed a little Dutch boy
    b. Mythical Frankish king who could serve as a role model for James II
    c. State with power enough to keep order
    d. Ancient political principle of the right to revolution
    e. New invention that would make British ships more dependable

18. All of the following are true of seventeenth century culture *except*

    a. Bernini completed Saint Peter's Basilica
    b. Rembrandt left an immense fortune to medical science
    c. Lope de Vega wrote plays that he knew would please the public
    d. Racine used classical themes for his contemporary plays
    e. Molière satirized the religious and social practices of France

19. One of the best examples of Baroque art is

    a. El Greco's Toledo Altarpiece
    b. Rembrandt's Scenes of Amsterdam
    c. Poussin's Classical Dreamworld
    d. Bernini's Interior of Saint Peter's Basilica
    e. Judith Leyster's Scenes from Peasant Life

20. Molière avoided legal harassment due to the

    a. Wealth and influence of his father
    b. Immense popularity of his plays
    c. Protection of Louis XIV
    d. Intervention of the Archbishop of Paris
    e. Use of Latin for phrases that might appear pornographic

Complete the Following Sentences

1. Henry IV had granted French Huguenots civil rights with his Edict of _____, but Louis XIV took them away with his Edict of _____.

2. Jean-Baptiste Colbert, controller-general of _____ for Louis XIV, followed the policy of _____, encouraging _____, discouraging _____.

3. The suspicion that France and Spain would be united when Louis XIV's _____ became the Spanish King Philip V, led to the War of the _____ _____.

4. The Hohenzollern ruler who built the Prussian state, the Great Elector _____ _____, based his structure on a large and efficient _____ _____ and used a _____ to raise revenues.

5. In Italy, the three arms of the Counter-Reformation, the _____, the _____, and the _____, long stifled all resistance to Catholic orthodoxy.

6. Peter Romanov decided after a trip to _____ Europe that Russia was a _____ _____ and needed an infusion of modern _____.

7. When it became evident to the English in 1688 that the baby son of King James II would perpetuate a _____ dynasty, they sent him into exile and chose as their monarchs William of _____ and his wife _____, the daughter of James II.

8. American and French used Englishman's John Locke's theories to demand _____ government, the rule of _____, and protection of _____.

9. The Golden Age of Dutch painting was financed by Dutch _____ and reached its zenith with the work of _____, who ironically in his later years eschewed _____ success.

10. In his play _____ Molière poked fun at the Paris _____, and in reaction they had it banned from the stage for _____ years.

Place the Following in Chronological Order and Give Dates

1.	Peter Romanov's trip to the West	1.
2.	War of the Spanish Succession	2.
3.	Turkish siege of Vienna	3.
4.	England's Glorious Revolution	4.
5.	Publication of Hobbes' *Leviathan*	5.
6.	Michael Romanov begins his reign	6.
7.	Edict of Fontainebleau	7.

Questions for Critical Thought

1. Outline the theory of Absolutism as propounded by Bodin and Bossuet; then illustrate how it worked, using Louis XIV's France as your example.

2. Describe in detail the life of the aristocracy at Louis XIV's court in Versailles. To what extent was Louis master and to what extent a slave of his court?

3. What factors transformed the small German province of Brandenburg-Prussia into the core of what was to be a German nation? Explain each factor.

4. Describe Peter Romanov's role in the emergence of modern Russia. Was he more or less important for Russia than Louis XIV was for France? Was he more or less absolute than Louis? Explain your answer.

5. Name the European nations that became either limited monarchies or republics rather than absolute monarchies. In each case explain why it developed as it did—and did not remain absolutist.

6. Explain what made the Dutch so commercially successful in the seventeenth century. Why did so few other nations find such success? Give examples.

7. Describe the way a nearly absolute monarchy evolved into the world's first constitutional monarchy in Britain. What persons and events contributed to this change, and what part did each play?

8. List and explain the various political theories that grew out of the Age of Absolutism. Show how each one was a product of its specific time and place.

Analysis of Primary Source Documents

1. Explain how and why Suzanne Gaudry was condemned to death. What do her trial and the verdict that ended it say about French law and society in her day?

2. Describe the treatment of peasants on the farm captured by foreign soldiers during the Thirty Years' War, as recounted in the novel *Simplicius Simplicissimus*. To what extent do you see exaggeration for effect, and to what extent does this account agree with what you have read of treatment of civilians in other wars?

3. Do Louis XIV's *Memoirs* show that he had given the duties of a king a lot or little thought? How well did his advice fit his own actions?

4. From Saint-Simon's account of Louis XIV's life, what do you conclude about the king's attitude toward other people, in particular women?

5. Explain how Peter Romanov's treatment of the rebellious Streltsy could be used to demonstrate Machiavelli's notion that the effective ruler must act without consideration for the usual principles of morality.

6. Explain how the 1688 British Bill of Rights paved the way for constitutional government in that kingdom. Show how this Bill influenced American colonists in the next century.

7. How much of Shakespeare's tribute to England in "Richard II" is patriotism, how much xenophobia, and how much the dramatist's wish to please his audience? Give examples of your opinion.

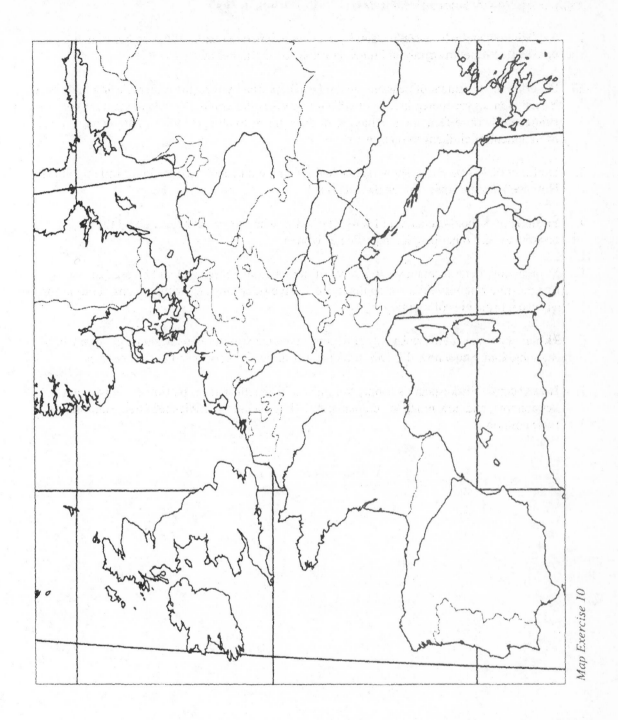

Map Exercise 10

Chapter 15

Map Exercise 10: Europe in 1648

Shade and label the following

1. Bavaria
2. Bohemia
3. Brandenburg
4. Denmark
5. Estonia
6. Hungary
7. Ottoman Empire
8. Poland
9. Portugal
10. Prussia
11. Russia
12. Sweden
13. Swiss Confederation
14. Tuscany
15. United Provinces

Pinpoint and label the following

1. Amsterdam
2. Berlin
3. Budapest
4. Danzig
5. Naples
6. Paris
7. Venice
8. Vienna
9. Warsaw

CHAPTER 16
TOWARD A NEW HEAVEN AND A NEW EARTH: THE SCIENTIFIC REVOLUTION AND THE EMERGENCE OF MODERN SCIENCE

Chapter Outline

I.   Background to the Scientific Revolution
    A.   Ancient Authors and Renaissance Artists
    B.   Technological Innovations and Mathematics
    C.   Renaissance Magic

II.   Toward a New Heaven: A Revolution in Astronomy
    A.   Copernicus
        1.   *On the Revolutions of the Heavenly Spheres*
        2.   Heliocentric Model
        3.   Church Reaction to Copernicus
    B.   Tycho Brahe
    C.   Johannes Kepler
    D.   Galileo and Controversy
        1.   Galileo's Telescope
        2.   *The Starry Messenger*
        3.   Inquisition
        4.   Laws of Motion
    E.   Isaac Newton and Universal Physics
        1.   *Principia*
        2.   Universal Law of Gravitation

III. Advances in Medicine and Chemistry
    A.   Paracelsus
        1.   Medicine as Chemistry
        2.   "Like Cures Like"
    B.   Andreas Vesalius
        1.   Human Dissection
        2.   Correction of Galen
    C.   William Harvey and the Human Blood System
    D.   Chemistry

IV.   Women in the Origins of Modern Science
    A.   Margaret Cavendish
    B.   Maria Merian and Entomology
    C.   Maria Winklemann
        1.   Discovery of a Comet
        2.   Rejection by the Berlin Academy
    D.   Debates on the Nature of Women
        1.   Male Agreement about Female Inferiority
        2.   Diminished Medical Role for Women

V.   Toward a New Earth: Descartes, Rationalism, and a New View of Humankind
    A.   Descartes' *Discourse on Method*
        1.   Rejection of the Senses
        2.   Separation of Mind and Matter
    B.   Implications of Cartesian Dualism

VI.   Scientific Method
    A.   The Scientific Method
        1.   Francis Bacon
        2.   Descartes
    B.   Spread of Scientific Knowledge
        1.   Scientific Societies
            a.   Royal Society of England
            b.   Royal Academy of France
            c.   Scientific Journals
        2.   Science and Society
            a.   Acceptance through Practicality
            b.   Science As a Means of Economic Progress and Social Stability
    C.   Science and Religion
        1.   Spinoza
        2.   Pascal

Chapter Summary

At the same time that kings were consolidating power and seeking a new social order based on absolute rule, an intellectual revolution took place which changed learned people's views of the universe, man's nature, and even the nature of truth itself. This revolution in science provided new models for heaven and for earth.

The Scientific Revolution began in the field of astronomy, and conclusions drawn by mathematicians and observers like Copernicus, Kepler, Galileo, and Newton both provided new understandings of the universe and its laws and called into question the wisdom of ancient and medieval scholars. Inspired by this study of astronomy and the realization that by empirical observation one can learn new things about the universe, scholars questioned and revised their opinions about medicine and the human sciences.

With the revolution in empirical studies came a new emphasis on human reason. Started by Rene Descartes and his famous *Discourse on Method*, the claims for rationalism focused attention on the nature and capacities of man's mind. While empiricism and rationalism were at times in conflict, they eventually merged to create a scholarship that rejected both tradition and authority in favor of continual reevaluation of established knowledge.

Religious doctrines were challenged and religious sensitivities ruffled by these secular endeavors, and scientists often found themselves at odds with religious powers. Even some of the scientists themselves were disturbed by the results of their studies. Pascal sought to reconcile science and religion, but his life was too brief to develop his ideas fully.

Yet science was too careful about its conclusions to be discredited and too useful to the world to be silenced. Scientific societies, sponsored by kings who saw benefits to their ambitions in science's achievements, disseminated amazing new discoveries and the general public enjoyed the fruits of scientific research. The modern world of progress and doubt was on its way.

Learning Objectives

1. Be able to trace the development of the science of astronomy from the work of Copernicus through that of Kepler, Galileo, and Newton.

2. Be able to trace the development of the science of medicine from its early, primitive day through the discoveries of Paracelsus, Vesalius, and Harvey.

3. Be able to explain the role that women played in the early years of modern science, recalling the obstacles that faced them.

4. Be able to describe the competition between science and religion in the seventeenth century, and account for their inability to find common ground as Pascal longed to see.

5. Be able to discuss the new scientific method of learning, the role of the scientific societies on its growth and influence, and the impact it had on European society.

Glossary of Names and Terms

1. Hermeticism: a belief that the world is a living embodiment of the divine and a magic-mathematical study the physical world can lead to God.

2. "Music of the Spheres": an early modern concept that creation, as demonstrated through its laws, has a harmony.

3. *Principia*: The work of Newton that captured and systematized all the laws of mechanics known to his day.

4. Paracelsus: early medical pioneer who believed that "like cures like" and gave drugs, often toxins, to his patients and kept records of his experiments.

5. Vesalius: medical pioneer who publicly dissected cadavers and published his findings in his book *On the Fabric of the Human Body*.

6. Margaret Cavendish: an aristocratic British woman scientist who, despite her recognized achievements, was excluded from the Royal Society on the basis of her gender.

7. *Querelles des femmes*: literally "arguments about women," from the debates held by male scientists over whether women should be accepted as academic and professional equals.

8. Francis Bacon: called for a total reconstruction of human knowledge, based now on scientific principles, which he gave concrete form.

9. Pascal: French mathematician who began but did not live to complete a work called *Pensees*, which he hoped could and would bridge the gap he saw growing between science and religion.

10. *Journal des Savants*: magazine of new scientific discoveries issued by the French Royal Academy of Sciences, which helped members keep up with each other's work.

Match the Following Words with their Definitions

1. Nicholas Copernicus

2. Tycho Brahe

3. Johannes Kepler

4. *The Starry Messenger*

5. Isaac Newton

6. William Harvey

7. Maria Winkelmann

8. Rene Descartes

9. *Pensées*

10. Royal Academy of Sciences

A. Advocated a geometric universe and tried to discover the "music of the spheres"

B. Discovered the circulation of blood and showed it was caused by the pumping of the heart

C. Astronomer denied a post in the Berlin Academy

D. Made astronomical observations from an island given him by the King of Denmark

E. Attempted to reconcile science and religion

F. Louis IV's contribution to the French scientific revolution

G. President of the Royal Society and only scientist buried in Westminster Abbey

H. Regarded Ptolemy's geocentric universe as too complicated

I. Advocate of rationalism who began his method with doubt

J. Defended Copernicus' system

Choose the Correct Answer

1. The Scientific Revolution of the seventeenth century was

    a. Stimulated by a new interest in Galen and Aristotle
    b. A direct result of the revolt against social conditions in the Middle Ages
    c. Born in the Augustinian monasteries
    d. More a gradual building on the accomplishments of previous centuries than a sudden shift in thought
    e. The cause of consternation among the kings of Europe

2. The greatest achievements in science during the sixteenth and seventeenth centuries came in the areas of

    a. Astronomy, mechanics, and medicine
    b. Astronomy, biology, and chemistry
    c. Biology, mechanics, and ballistics
    d. Engineering, physics, and dentistry
    e. Anatomy, engineering, and medicine

3. The general conception of the universe prior to Copernicus held that

    a. Heaven was at the center and all creation circled it
    b. The earth was at a stationary center, orbited by perfect crystalline spheres
    c. The earth rested on the shell of a giant turtle
    d. It was all a mystery known only to theologians
    e. To ask questions about it might threaten the Christian faith

4. Although he made deductions about the construction of the universe, Copernicus was by formal training a

    a. Mathematician, specializing in Calculus
    b. Banker attached to the Medici of Florence
    c. Cloistered Augustinian monk
    d. Military adviser to his uncle, an archbishop
    e. Canon (church) lawyer

5. The universal theories proposed by Copernicus

    a. Led to his arrest and imprisonment in a monastery
    b. Were supported by Protestants in order to make Catholics look provincial
    c. Made the universe less complicated by discarding Ptolemy's epicycle theory
    d. Explained the appearance of the sun's rotation with a theory of earthly rotation
    e. Were later completely discredited by Newton

6. Johannes Kepler believed that the truth of the universe could be found by combining the study of mathematics with that of

    a. Neoplatonic magic
    b. Greek literary symbolism
    c. The Book of Revelation
    d. The Book of Daniel
    e. Papal dispensations

7. Galileo held that the planets were

    a. Composed of material much like that of earth
    b. Reflections of the divine city
    c. Spheres composed of pure energy
    d. Merely mirages in the "desert" of space
    e. Inhabited by creatures made by a rival to God

8. Isaac Newton's scientific discoveries

    a. Were met with great hostility from the Church of England
    b. Formed the basis for universal physics until well into the twentieth century
    c. Completely divorced God from the universe and its laws
    d. Were the first to be printed in a language other than Latin
    e. Alienated him both from the Royal Society and the English monarchy

9. Newton's universal law of gravity

    a. Offered an explanation for all motion in the universe
    b. Had little practical application to the questions of universal motion
    c. Showed that humans could never understand why God made things the way they are
    d. Seemed to indicate that the universe began with a "big bang"
    e. Was lifted almost word for word from Copernicus

10. Paracelsus revolutionized the world of medicine in the sixteenth century by

    a. Disproving Galen's theory of two blood systems
    b. Dissecting human rather than animal cadavers
    c. Treating diseases with his "like cures like" method
    d. Rejecting "Christian Chemistry" as taught in the universities of his day
    e. Injecting himself with germs to note their effects

11. The role of women in the Scientific Revolution was best characterized by

    a. The way scientific communities welcomed women as members
    b. Maria Merian's breakthroughs in astronomy
    c. The manner in which Margaret Cavendish debated science with men
    d. Maria Winkelmann's professorship in physics at the University of Berlin
    e. Spinoza's arguments for the full equal treatment of women

12. The overall effect of the Scientific Revolution on the *querelles des femmes* was to

    a. Dispel old myths about female inferiority
    b. Increase the role of husbands in child care and education
    c. Justify the continuation of male dominance in the field
    d. Demonstrate that there was no inherent skeletal differences between the sexes
    e. Break down old walls and permit women their proper place in the field

13. Maria Merian introduced to the field of science the importance of

    a. Sterilizing surgical instruments
    b. Viewing heavenly bodies through smoked lenses rather than with the naked eye
    c. Reconciling scientific findings with theological principles
    d. Not judging a person's work by his or her gender
    e. Providing precise illustrations of her subjects

14. Francis Bacon was important to the Scientific Revolution because of his emphasis on

    a. Experimentation and inductive reasoning
    b. Pure, theoretical reasoning
    c. Deductive conclusions, which moved from general to particular principles
    d. The obligation of scientists to protect nature
    e. Reconciling science with religion

15. Organized religion in the seventeenth century

    a. Conceded that only science can explain the universe
    b. Rejected scientific discoveries that conflicted with Christian theology's view of the universe
    c. Cooperated as an equal and willing partner to the study of science
    d. Simply ignored science, calling it a new "toy for the minds of God's children"
    e. Tried to imprison every scientist who threatened the faith

16. During the seventeenth century, royal and princely patronage of science

    a. Declined as science turned more and more to medicine
    b. Was strongest in Italy and Spain
    c. Became an international phenomenon
    d. Replaced church funding of scientific research
    e. Put severe limits on the scope of scientific experimentation

17. The scientific societies established the first

    a. Fundraising events for medical research
    b. Journals describing the discoveries of members
    c. Codes of ethics for the treatment of animals
    d. Codes of ethics for the treatment of humans
    e. Endowed chairs of science in the universities

18. Science became an integral part of Western culture in the eighteenth century because

    a. People came to see it as the only way to find the truth
    b. Its mechanistic theories were popular with kings
    c. Radical groups like the Levellers, when they came to power, insisted on the adoption of scientific laws
    d. It offered a new means of making profit and maintaining social order
    e. There was no alternative to its good sense

19. Spinoza said that man's failure to understand the true nature of God leads to

    a. A false worship of nature
    b. A society in which men use nature for selfish purposes
    c. A decline in the powers of moral judgment
    d. Sexual permissiveness
    e. Slavish devotion, exemplified by monastic deprivation

20. Blaise Pascal believed that

    a. Man can know God through pure reason
    b. Man is the summation of all things
    c. Christians should trust only what God has revealed in Scripture
    d. God can be known only by the heart, not the reason
    e. Faith and reason would find resolution given enough time

Complete the Following Sentences

1. Renaissance humanists demonstrated that not all ancient scholars had agreed with
    _____, _____, and _____, even though these men were
    accepted without question by medieval science.

2. Early modern scientists agreed with Leonardo da Vinci that since God eternally
    _____, nature is inherently _____; yet these same scientists looked
    for the secrets of the universe through _____ magic.

3. Copernicus rejected Ptolemy's _____ universe and postulated a
    _____ one because he found Ptolemy's system too _____.

4. Peering through his telescope, Galileo discovered _____ on the moon, Jupiter's
    four _____, and _____ spots.

5. Galileo explained the three approaches people might take to the new astronomy in his
    Dialogue, where three characters, _____, _____, and
    _____ argued the theory of Copernicus.

6. During eighteen months in his home village, Isaac Newton invented _____,
    developed theories about the composition of _____, and began formulating the
    universal law of _____.

7. Vesalius disputed Galen's assertion that blood vessels originate in the _____ but did not doubt his claim that two different kinds of blood flow through the _____ and _____.

8. Descartes argued that man's _____ cannot be doubted but that the reality of the _____ _____ can and should be, thus creating what came to be called Cartesian _____.

9. Although he was expelled from his Amsterdam _____ for heresy, Spinoza was actually a _____, not the atheist his critics claimed, believing that all things are in _____.

10. The Royal Society was chartered in 1662 by _____, while the Royal Academy of Sciences was recognized in 1666 by _____. Both emphasized the _____ value of scientific research.

Place the Following in the Order of their Publications and Give Dates

1. Harvey's *On the Motion of the*   1.
   Heart and Blood

2. Newton's *Principia*   2.

3. Copernicus' *On the Revolutions of the*   3.
   Heavenly Spheres

4. Bacon's *The Great Instauration*   4.

5. Descartes' *Discourse on Method*   5.

6. Pascal's *Pensées*   6.

7. Galileo's *The Starry Messenger*   7.

Questions for Critical Thought

1. Discuss the causes of the Scientific Revolution of the seventeenth century. Of these causes, which seems strangest to modern minds? Why?

2. What did the discoveries in seventeenth century astronomy contribute to the Scientific Revolution? What did each of the major astronomers add to the field?

3. What three men contributed the most knowledge to the field of medicine during the seventeenth century? Briefly describe each one's contribution.

4. Describe the contribution women made to the Scientific Revolution. Why did male scientists have such difficulties accepting them as equals?

5. Discuss the ways in which scientific discoveries affected the seventeenth century's image of man. How did the new image differ from the old one?

6. Describe the "scientific method" that developed in the seventeenth century, and show how it was used in one of the emerging branches of science.

7. How did the Scientific Revolution affect religious thought? How did religious thought affect the Revolution?

8. What role did monarchs play in the Scientific Revolution? What were their motivations, and to what extent were their expectations realized?

Analysis of Primary Source Documents

1. Show how Copernicus' heliocentric theory was at the same time so simple and so profound.

2. Describe the "tone" of the famous correspondence between Kepler and Galileo. How can you explain the apparent absence of jealousy usually associated with famous men?

3. What personality traits can you find in Galileo's account of his astronomical observations that would explain why he was a successful scientist?

4. Compare Galileo's argument that his scientific theory did not threaten the Christian religion with Bellarmine's contention that Galileo's ideas would damage the holy faith. Is it possible for a modern person to see both sides of this issue?

5. Show how Isaac Newton's four rules of reasoning are the end result of two centuries in which the "scientific method" was developed and refined.

6. Speculate on why—amid the scientific progress of his century and despite evidence to the contrary—Spinoza was so unprepared to accept women as equals.

7. To what degree do you find Descartes' method for finding truth a good guide? Point out any difficulties one might meet applying it to contemporary scientific problems.

8. What was at the root of Pascal's doubts about man's ability to find scientific certainty? What problems for science in the future did he accurately predict?

ANSWER KEY

CHAPTER 1

Matching

1. I
2. F
3. D
4. A
5. J
6. H
7. C
8. B
9. E
10. G

Multiple Choice

1. d
2. e
3. b
4. c
5. b
6. a
7. b
8. e
9. c
10. c
11. b
12. b
13. a
14. a
15. a
16. b
17. b
18. b
19. e
20. a

Completion

1. Turkey, surpluses, weapons, jewelry
2. Irrigating, drainage ditches
3. Priests, Kings
4. Severe, social class
5. Continuity, cyclical
6. Four, two, three

Answer Key

7. Nomes, nomarchs, pharaoh, vizier
8. Osiris, Seth, Isis
9. Old, Giza, 2540
10. His Majesty, beard

Chronology

1. Çatal Hüyük: 6700-5700 B.C.
2. Great Pyramid: 2540 B.C.
3. Stonehenge: 2100-1900 B.C.
4. Hammurabi: 1792-1750 B.C.
5. Hyksos: ca. 1630-1567 B.C.
6. Tutmosis III: 1480-1450 B.C.
7. Tell-el-Amarna: 1364-1347 B.C.

CHAPTER 2

Matching

1. J
2. H
3. G
4. I
5. A
6. E
7. C
8. B
9. F
10. D

Multiple Choice

1. e
2. a
3. b
4. d
5. c
6. a
7. d
8. b
9. d
10. a
11. b
12. d
13. c
14. c
15. b

16. c
17. b
18. b
19. e
20. c

Completion

1. Temple, Ark, Covenant
2. Egypt, Babylon, Cyrus
3. Yahweh, covenant, law
4. Phoenicians, alphabet
5. King, absolute
6. Iron, guerilla, terrorize
7. Media, Lydia, Ionian, Babylon
8. Egypt, Cambyses, Memphis
9. Darius, Susa, Persepolis
10. Zoroaster, *Yasna*, Ahuramazda, Ahriman

Chronology

1. Exodus: 1300-1200 B.C.
2. David: 1000-970 B.C.
3. Building of Solomon's temple: 970-930 B.C.
4. Northern Kingdom of Israel destroyed by the Assyrians: 722 B.C.
5. Zoroaster: 660 B.C.
6. Fall of Jerusalem: 586 B.C.
7. Cyrus: 550-530 B.C.

CHAPTER 3

Matching

1. D
2. G
3. A
4. J
5. B
6. F
7. C
8. I
9. E
10. H

Answer Key

Multiple Choice

1. b
2. b
3. e
4. b
5. c
6. b
7. a
8. b
9. c
10. e
11. c
12. b
13. a
14. d
15. c
16. c
17. b
18. d
19. c
20. a

Completion

1. Troy, Achilles, battlefield
2. Military, seven, twenty
3. 10, 500, democracy
4. Sparta, Athens, Peloponnesian War
5. Pericles, democracy, empire
6. Rational, human beings, gods
7. Parthenon, Acropolis, Athena
8. Corrupting, youth, death
9. Democracy, ideal, *Republic*
10. Father, husband, son

Chronology

1. Mycenaean Civilization: 1400-1200 B.C.
2. *Iliad*: 750 B.C.
3. Solon's reforms: 594ff B.C.
4. Battle of Marathon: 490 B.C.
5. Parthenon: 447-432 B.C.
6. Peloponnesian War: 431-404 B.C.
7. Death of Socrates: 399 B.C.

CHAPTER 4

Matching

1. J
2. E
3. F
4. H
5. I
6. D
7. A
8. G
9. C
10. B

Multiple Choice

1. c
2. b
3. c
4. a
5. c
6. d
7. d
8. c
9. a
10. c
11. b
12. b
13. a
14. c
15. c
16. d
17. e
18. b
19. b
20. c

Completion

1. Gaugamela, Darius, cavalry
2. Marry native, Stateira, Roxane
3. Ptolemy, Seleucus, Antigonus
4. Infantry, cavalry, elephants
5. Abandoned, pirates, prisoners of war
6. Education, pay, gold crown
7. Alexandria, 500,000 systematic
8. 40, Mediterranean, Rome
9. Science, philosophy, astronomy, geometry
10. Epicureanism, Stoicism

Answer Key

Chronology

1. Reign of Philip II: 359-336 B.C.
2. Battle of Issus: 333 B.C.
3. Battle of Gaugamela: 331 B.C.
4. Death of Alexander: 323 B.C.
5. Death of Epicurus: 270 B.C.
6. Birth of Polybius: 203 B.C.
7. Maccabaean uprising: 164 B.C.

CHAPTER 5

Matching

1. D
2. H
3. F
4. G
5. A
6. B
7. E
8. C
9. J
10. I

Multiple Choice

1. c
2. a
3. c
4. b
5. c
6. b
7. c
8. a
9. a
10. c
11. c
12. d
13. c
14. c
15. c
16. d
17. b
18. a
19. c
20. a

Completion

1. Seven, Latium, Tiber
2. Axe, rods, power
3. *Paterfamilias*, gens
4. Plebian, plebians, patricians
5. Delaying, North Africa
6. Greek, Macedonia, Corinth
7. Divine Law, state, gods
8. Greek, bilingual
9. Bridges, aqueducts, concrete
10. Stock, masks, stock

Chronology

1. Twelve Tables: 450 B.C.
2. Roman Confederation: 338 B.C.
3. First Punic War: 264-241 B.C.
4. First Macedonian War: 215-205 B.C.
5. Consulships of Marius: 107-100 B.C.
6. Caesar's Assassination: 44 B.C.
7. Octavian defeats Antony: 31 B.C.

CHAPTER 6

Matching

1. I
2. G
3. F
4. A
5. C
6. J
7. H
8. B
9. E
10. D

Multiple Choice

1. e
2. c
3. c
4. b
5. d
6. c
7. a
8. b
9. c
10. e

11. a
12. b
13. c
14. a
15. b
16. a
17. d
18. d
19. c
20. b

Completion

1.   *Res Gestae*, bronze pillars
2.   Julius Caesar, Augustus, Roma
3.   *The Art of Love*, sexual, upper class
4.   Moral lessons, medicine, sick
5.   Alexandria, Ephesus, Antioch
6.   Pliny the Younger, villas, digestion
7.   Divine plan, humanity, simply
8.   Coliseum, public slaughter
9.   Gladiatorial doctor, court physician
10. Roman, Tarsus, universal foundation

Chronology

1.   Death of Augustus: 14 A.D.
2.   Jesus' Sermon on the Mount: ca 28-30
3.   Jewish revolt: 66
4.   Four emperors: 69
5.   Eruption of Vesuvius: 79
6.   Marcus Aurelius reign: 161-180
7.   Persecution of Decius: 249-51

CHAPTER 7

Matching

1.   E
2.   H
3.   F
4.   C
5.   J
6.   D
7.   G
8.   A
9.   B
10. I

Multiple Choice

1. b
2. d
3. d
4. a
5. c
6. b
7. c
8. a
9. c
10. a
11. d
12. c
13. a
14. b
15. a
16. c
17. d
18. c
19. a
20. e

Completion

1. Oath, oath helpers, divine intervention
2. Nicaea, Arianism, same substance
3. Temporal power, England, Germany
4. Rule, Benedict, moderation
5. Columba, Iona, Angles, Saxons
6. Celtic, Roman, fusion
7. *City of God*, government, history
8. Law code, Hagia Sophia
9. Religious images, idolatry
10. Mecca, Medina, Hegira

Chronology

1. Visigoths sack Rome: 410
2. Odoacer deposes Romulus Augustulus: 476
3. Clovis converted: ca 500
4. Justinian codifies Roman law: 529-33
5. Hagia Sophia completed: 537
6. Bede completes *History*: 731
7. Martel defeats Muslims: 732

CHAPTER 8

Matching

1. C
2. G
3. F
4. H
5. J
6. I
7. A
8. D
9. B
10. E

Multiple Choice

1. d
2. b
3. c
4. d
5. a
6. d
7. a
8. a
9. c
10. b
11. b
12. a
13. c
14. d
15. c
16. b
17. a
18. c
19. d
20. c

Completion

1. Einhard, fierce, devils
2. Charlemagne, Leo III, Rome
3. Miniscule, printing, Merovingian
4. Charles, Louis, Lothair
5. Sicily, Hungary, Normandy
6. Alfred, Wessex, southern
7. Nicene, Photius, schism
8. Rus, Novgorod, Kiev
9. Vladimir, Byzantine, religious, imperial, Byzantium
10. Mathematics, astronomy, and medicine

Chronology

1. Reign of Pepin: 751-68
2. Charlemagne crowned emperor: 800
3. Conquest of Saxons: 804
4. Michael III begins to reign in Byzantium: 842
5. Treaty of Verdun: 843
6. Alfred makes peace with Danes: 886
7. Vladimir's conversion to Christianity: 987

CHAPTER 9

Matching

1. G
2. D
3. J
4. A
5. C
6. I
7. B
8. F
9. E
10. H

Multiple Choice

1. c
2. a
3. b
4. c
5. d
6. d
7. a
8. d
9. c
10. c
11. b
12. a
13. a
14. b
15. c
16. d
17. b
18. a
19. b
20. c

Answer Key

Completion

1. *Aratum, carruca*, drain
2. Christmas, Easter, Pentecost, saints, Virgin Mary
3. Noble family, defensible fortress
4. Louis VII, crusade, Henry II, sons
5. Charters, communes
6. Mayor, ale, independence
7. Apprentice, master craftsman, journeyman, masterpiece
8. Bologna, Paris, Oxford, lecture
9. Scholastic, Heloise, castrated
10. *Summa Theologica*, 600, dialectical method

Chronology

1. Laon revolt: 1116
2. Suger's find: 1140
3. Abelard dies: 1142
4. Bologna founded: 1158
5. Eleanor's sons revolt: 1173-74
6. Oxford founded: 1208
7. Aquinas dies: 1274

CHAPTER 10

Matching

1. B
2. G
3. E
4. I
5. F
6. A
7. C
8. D
9. J
10. H

Multiple Choice

1. e
2. a
3. d
4. a
5. d
6. c
7. b
8. b
9. e
10. a

11. b
12. a
13. b
14. d
15. d
16. c
17. b
18. c
19. a
20. e

Completion

1. William, Normandy, Harold Godwinson
2. *Magna Carta*, Runnymeade
3. Great Council, knights, residents
4. Christian, Muslim, Jewish
5. Novgorod, Mongols, Germans, Moscow
6. Gregory VII, Henry IV, invest
7. Sun, moon, superior
8. Clare, Poor Clares, poverty
9. Pure, light, darkness
10. Jews, homosexuals

Chronology

1. Battle of Hastings: 1066
2. First Crusade: 1096-99
3. Becket murdered: 1170
4. *Magna Carta* signed: 1215
5. Mongols conquer Russia: 1230's
6. Crusades end: 1291
7. First French Estates-General meets: 1302

Chapter 11

Matching

1. B
2. G
3. F
4. D
5. I
6. H
7. E
8. J
9. A
10. C

Answer Key

Multiple Choice

1. c
2. b
3. c
4. b
5. a
6. c
7. b
8. c
9. e
10. d
11. a
12. b
13. b
14. d
15. c
16. d
17. a
18. c
19. e
20. a

Completion

1. Asia, rats, 25, 50
2. Wat Tyler, John Ball, poll tax
3. Poitiers, Agincourt, Calais
4. Emperor, four, three
5. *Unam Sanctam*, Anagni, Avignon
6. Marsiglio, Padua, conciliarism, community, faithful
7. Meister Eckhart, Gerhard Groote, Common Life
8. Virgil, Beatrice, Saint Bernard
9. *Canterbury Tales*, Southwark, Thomas Becket
10. Humors, herbal, bloodletting

Chronology

1. *Unam Sanctam*: 1302
2. Hundred Years' War begins: 1337
3. Jacquerie crushed: 1358
4. Great Schism begins: 1378
5. Battle of Agincourt: 1415
6. Joan of Arc leads French: 1429-31
7. End of Hundred Years War: 1453

CHAPTER 12

Matching

1. D
2. I
3. F
4. A
5. H
6. B
7. J
8. C
9. E
10. G

Multiple Choice

1. d
2. a
3. b
4. c
5. e
6. b
7. b
8. c
9. a
10. a
11. d
12. a
13. b
14. c
15. b
16. d
17. b
18. a
19. c
20. b

Completion

1. Medici, bankers, French
2. *Courtier*, aristocracy, grace
3. Ferrara, Mantua, library
4. Florence, *The Prince,* morality
5. Petrarch, Pico della Mirandola, unlimited
6. Leonardo, Michelangelo, Raphael
7. Urbino, Julius II, Saint Peter
8. Eye, power, distinction
9. Jews, Muslims, Most Catholic
10. Julius II, Sixtus IV, Alexander VI

Chronology

1. End of Great Schism: 1417
2. Pragmatic Sanction of Bourges: 1438
3. Fall of Constantinople: 1453
4. Marriage of Ferdinand and Isabella: 1469
5. Bosworth Field: 1485
6. Expulsion of the Jews: 1492
7. Sack of Rome: 1527

CHAPTER 13

Matching

1. F
2. I
3. A
4. J
5. D
6. C
7. H
8. B
9. G
10. E

Multiple Choice

1. c
2. a
3. c
4. a
5. b
6. a
7. d
8. e
9. d
10. c
11. d
12. b
13. a
14. c
15. b
16. b
17. e
18. a
19. a
20. b

Completion

1.   *Utopia*, divorce, Henry VIII
2.   Augustinian, indulgences, Ninety-five
3.   Princes, peasants, gospel
4.   Switzerland, Germany, Lord's Supper
5.   Melchiorites, Munster, New Jerusalem
6.   Catherine, Anne Boleyn, Edward VI
7.   *Institutes of the Christian Religion*, sovereignty, predestination
8.   Wives, mothers, Eve
9.   Huguenot, Catholic, France
10. Catholics, Mary, beheaded

Chronology

1.   Diet of Worms: 1521
2.   Schmalkaldic League formed: 1531
3.   English Act of Supremacy: 1534
4.   Calvin's *Institutes* published: 1536
5.   Society of Jesus recognized: 1540
6.   Council of Trent convenes: 1545
7.   Spanish Armada: 1588

CHAPTER 14

Matching

1.   B
2.   J
3.   E
4.   C
5.   I
6.   H
7.   F
8.   D
9.   A
10. G

Multiple Choice

1.   d
2.   b
3.   b
4.   c
5.   e
6.   a
7.   c
8.   b
9.   c
10. d

11. a
12. b
13. a
14. c
15. d
16. c
17. b
18. d
19. b
20. a

Completion

1. Navigator, Vasco da Gama, de Albuquerque
2. Hernando Cortes, Francesco Pizarro, de Las Casas
3. Laborers, protect, spiritual
4. 300, 450, 100, 10
5. Bengal, 3,000, Plassey
6. Macartney, Canton, Qianlong
7. Missionaries, Nagasaki, three
8. Legislatures, resented, resisted
9. Unchangeable, war, expense
10. Cattle, cane sugar, maize

Chronology

1. Dias around Africa: 1488
2. Tordesillas: 1494
3. First slaves to America: 1518
4. Champlain in Quebec: 1608
5. Dutch seize Malacca: 1641
6. Plassey: 1757
7. French cede Canada: 1763

CHAPTER 15

Matching

1. J
2. H
3. G
4. C
5. B
6. E
7. A
8. D
9. I
10. F

Multiple Choice

1. d
2. b
3. d
4. c
5. a
6. b
7. c
8. a
9. b
10. a
11. d
12. c
13. a
14. a
15. b
16. a
17. c
18. b
19. d
20. c

Completion

1. Nantes, Fontainebleau
2. Finances, mercantilism, export, import
3. Grandson, Spanish Succession
4. Frederick William, standing army, Commissariat
5. Inquisition, Index, Jesuits
6. Western, backward, technology
7. Catholic, Orange, Mary
8. Constitutional, law, rights
9. Commerce, Rembrandt, materialistic
10. *Tartuffe*, clergy, five

Chronology

1. Michael Romanov begins reign: 1613
2. *Leviathan* published: 1651
3. Turkish siege of Vienna: 1683
4. Edict of Fontainebleau: 1685
5. England's Glorious Revolution: 1688
6. Peter Romanov's trip to the West: 1697-98
7. War of Spanish Succession: 1702-1713

CHAPTER 16

Matching

1. H
2. D
3. A
4. J
5. G
6. B
7. C
8. I
9. E
10. F

Multiple Choice

1. d
2. a
3. b
4. e
5. d
6. a
7. a
8. b
9. a
10. c
11. c
12. c
13. e
14. a
15. b
16. c
17. b
18. d
19. b
20. d

Completion

1. Aristotle, Galen, Ptolemy
2. Geometrizes, mathematical, Hermetic
3. Geocentric, Heliocentric, complicated
4. Mountains, moons, sun
5. Simplicio, Sagredo, Salviati
6. Calculus, light, gravity
7. Liver, veins, arteries
8. Mind, material world, Dualism
9. Synagogue, panentheist, God
10. Charles II, Louis XIV, practical

Chronology

1. Copernicus' *Revolutions*: 1543
2. Gilileo's *Messenger*: 1610
3. Bacon's *Instauration*: 1620
4. Harvey's *Motion*: 1628
5. Descartes' *Method*: 1637
6. Pascal's *Pensées*: 1669
7. Newton's *Principia*: 1687